T TADWEEN PUBLISHING

Tadween Publishing, a new form of "publishing house," is part of the *Arab Studies Institute*, an umbrella institute that has run four organizations since 1992: the peer-reviewed publication, *Arab Studies Journal*, the electronic publication, *Jadaliyya*, the research institute, *FAMA* (Forum on Arab and Muslim Affairs), and the documentary collective, *Quilting Point*.

Middle East Studies Pedagogy Initiative (MESPI)

In cooperation with the Middle East Studies Program at George Mason University, Tadween is launching the Middle East Studies Pedagogy Initiative (MESPI) to provide critical, user-friendly, and informative pedagogical material and instruction to educators in the field and beyond. MESPI will build on two counts: Educators Networks and Pedagogical Resources. Tadween's Educators Network (TEN) provides members with complementary copies of Tadween Publications intended for the classroom. If you are an educator, please sign up to TEN here to receive your complimentary copies. MESPI will be producing Pedagogical Publications intended primarily for the classroom, covering various countries, topics, events, themes, and paradigms. Starting with our pilot project, JADMAG, these publications will be produced on a regular basis and will be accompanied by resources for further examination of the subject matter.

www.TADWEENPUBLISHING.com

JADMAG PEDAGOGY PUBLICATIONS ISSUE 4.2

What is Political Economy?

Contents

Participating members of the Political Economy Project and attendees of the Founding Workshop gather at George Mason University. Image from the Arab Studies Institute.

Political Economy Defined

Joel Beinin The brief essays presented here do not present a unanimous perspective, nor was it anticipated that they should. Indeed, several of the authors advance overtly contradictory positions on key issues. Wael Gamal, Bassam Haddad, Toufic Haddad, Adam Hanieh, and Mandy Turner place the epistemology and methodology of political economy firmly within the tradition of Marxian historical materialism and view it as an antidote both to various culturalist and textualist modes of analysis and to globally prevailing forms of domination and exploitation. More pointedly, Max Ajl argues that the central object of analysis for political economy is global capitalism.

Because there is no academic discipline that is dedicated to a wholistic study of capitalism, some authors (Ajl, B. Haddad, Hanieh) explicitly argue that the current disciplinary structure of academia—in particular the division between "politics" and "economics" (and, I would add, "sociology")—and the concepts rooted in these intellectual and institutional structures subvert the critical political economy we seek to advance. Others (Melani Cammett and Pete Moore) are willing to deploy concepts and methods derived from liberal or new institutionalist versions of political economy. Gamal invokes Antonio Gramsci and Thomas Piketty in arguing that the "experts" of the international financial institutions, relying on mainstream economic analytic tools, will never solve the pressing problems of the Middle East. They regarded Tunisia and Egypt on the eve of the 2011 popular uprisings as "success stories." Their misjudgments reveal, yet again, that "expertise" is always already imbedded in hierarchies of power.

Aaron Jakes, by way of a critical review of Sven Beckert's *Empire of Cotton: A Global History*, argues that a narrow focus on the processes of capitalist production ignores consumption, which is necessarily a matter of culture and taste. Firat Bozçalı, in discussing the very material practices of smuggling oil and other commodities into Turkey from Syria and Iran, similarly draws our attention to the life cycles of commodities, the discourse of legitimation of illegal acts of smuggling, and the work of legal documents and court proceedings in constructing the meaning of smuggling. Jakes and Bozçalı would concur with Ahmad Shokr's warning that we should not ignore the insights of cultural studies, feminism, and postcolonial theory, lest we expose ourselves to the critiques they so powerfully directed against the "new social history" that emerged in the 1960s and entered Middle East and North African studies in the late 1970s. Jakes suggests that "politically committed intellectual generosity" may help to resolve the impasse created by the clash of culturalist forms of analysis and political economy. Hanieh proposes, following Bertell Ollman and David McNally, the theoretically more difficult proposition that all analytical and social categories are mutually constitutive. This is not at all incompatible with Jakes' formulation.

Gamal calls for dismantling the discourse of neoliberalism and formulating a counter-discourse. This recalls Karl Marx's proposition in *The German Ideology* that, "The ruling ideas are nothing more than the ideal expression of the dominant material relationships,

the dominant material relationships grasped as ideas." However, Marx, who was not as determinist as some culturalists dismissively assert, also maintained, in the introduction to the *Critique of Hegel's Philosophy of Right*, that theory (i.e., ideas) can become a material force. Consequently, the outcome of struggles between critical ideas and constituted forms of power is always open ended.

> *Political economy is necessarily interdisciplinary, whether conceived as the fusion of distinct disciplines or their negation.*

Despite the significant differences among them, the essays, while not unanimous, converge on several points:

1. Political economy is necessarily interdisciplinary, whether conceived as the fusion of distinct disciplines or their negation.

2. The intellectual genealogy of political economy draws on several theoretical traditions, although, as Omar Dahi and others suggest, the central strands of that genealogy run from Marx, to John Maynard Keynes, to Raoul Prebisch, Immanuel Wallerstein and dependency theory, to various neo-Marxian approaches such as the "social structures of accumulation" and "regulation" schools.

3. This intellectual genealogy naturally makes political economy a form of critique of existing disciplinary boundaries, conceptual categories, scholarly conventions, and structures of knowledge and power in the sense that this term was developed from the Frankfurt School to Michel Foucault.

4. Political economy is centrally concerned with institutions, relations of power, and social conflict.

5. Political economy understands the historical formation of capitalism—as a mode of production, a system of circulation and consumption of commodities, and a structure of power—on a global scale. States, markets, and classes must be simultaneously situated in their local, regional, and global contexts. It stands opposed to Eurocentrism and methodological nationalism and must be attentive to the social construction of space, national borders.

6. As Ajl, Gamal, B. Haddad, Hanieh, and Jakes articulate explicitly, but we would all agree, the critical political economy that we envision is allied to a politics of solidarity with our colleagues in the Middle East and with the popular struggles in the region. Let us proceed from these points of consensus.

Shana Marsall notes, as part of her explanation for why study of the political economy of the Middle East lacks the normal accouterments of academic subfields (e.g., canonical texts, a flagship peer-reviewed journal, endowed chairs, and postdoctoral fellowships), "In the beginning, Political Economy was 'all of' politics and very nearly 'all of' social science." That is, political economy

Participating members of The Political Economy Project gather at George Mason University. Image from the Arab Studies Institute.

emerged as a branch of moral philosophy seeking to understand the mutual interactions among commerce and the creation of wealth and law, social customs, political regimes, and the distribution of national wealth. Categories like race, gender, and empire were not central to political economy studies of the eighteenth and ninteenth centuries, but came to be so in the twentieth century.

If political economy and social history have been relatively underdeveloped in studies of Palestine in particular, as Charles Anderson argues, perhaps the reason is that the central issues in the conflict are perceived as political. Turner usefully turns our attention to the political economy of western aid in the Occupied Palestinian Territories since the 1993 Oslo Accords and its role in reproducing the simulacrum of statehood embodied in the Palestinian Authority. In any case, political economy was the theme of the 2014 first annual conference on New Directions in Palestinian Studies at Brown University. It featured many young scholars whose work has already begun making an impact.

A central concern of political economy has been class analysis. This means asking, as Cammett formulates the question, "Who gets what, when, and how," but it also entails analyzing how and to whose benefit structures of accumulation and distribution of social wealth are reproduced. B. Haddad notes that even in Syria, the ruling class had a "strong affinity" for neoliberal prescriptions despite its refusal to deal with the "unholy trinity"—the IMF, the World Bank, and the GATT. He underlines that the global context is essential to explaining this affinity.

Marx, like Adam Smith, analyzed the social structure of the accumulation of capital in the framework of national states. The advent of Marxian theories of imperialism (Rosa Luxemburg, Rudolf Hilferding, Vladimir Lenin, Nikolai Bukharin, etc.) in the early twentieth century and the flourishing of dependency theory in the mid-twentieth century directed the attention of political economy studies to larger frameworks. "Globalization" in much of contemporary usage can be understood as the term of the American ruling class and its partners, their stenographers, and international financial elites for what dependency theorists called the "world economy."

Scale of analysis is directly related to how we understand class structures. For example, "Occupy Wall Street" popularized the conception of a one percent class with interests opposed to those of the vast majority of Americans, the ninety-nine percent, within the territorial boundaries of the United States. This is very roughly true in an American national context, but inserting just one Middle East-related fact into the narrative—the United States, with about 4.4 percent of the world's population, consumes about nineteen percent of global energy resources—radically alters the story. Many ninty-nine percenters continue to participate in and reproduce what the Gulf Oil Company, in a popular billboard of the 1950s, called "the American way of life"—a largely white, suburbanized, automobile-based economy and culture that has destroyed our inner cities and their social and educational services and threatens to destroy the earth itself.

As several contributors note, the study of institutions is both a central concern of political economy and a hot topic in the disciplines of political science and economics. Laleh Khalili usefully defines institutions as "loci of politico-economic power" and places on her research agenda the study of their inner workings. Khalili and Pete Moore concur that Timur Kuran and Avner Greif raise important questions about the origins of the institutions that facilitate capital accumulation in the metropoles of the world capitalist market. However, oddly, for economists, they propose culturalist explanations for the Muslim world's failure to develop the requisite institutions to generate an economic takeoff. They leave us with reiterations of the thesis of Bernard Lewis's *What Went Wrong?: The Clash Between Islam and Modernity in the Middle East* or David Landes's *The Wealth and Poverty of Nations: Why Some Are So Rich and Some So Poor*.

Therefore, studying institutions is insufficient in and of itself. Institutions should be understood as the historical outcome of intersecting social struggles, not texts or "culture." Moreover, once established, institutions do not sustain themselves. There are constant struggles over their reproduction and legitimation. Those who benefit from existing hierarchies of power work hard to obscure them and make it appear that the existing order of things is "natural."

I would suggest that our efforts to recenter political economy as a mode of analysis for Middle East studies do not begin from a state of affairs that is as bad as Anderson and Marshall suggest. Political economy was an important element of the turn to social history in Middle East studies that was ascendant from the late 1970s to the late 1990s. The formative texts of that era were Hanna Batatu, *The Old Social Classes and the Revolutionary Movements of Iraq*; Ervand Abrahamian, *Iran Between Two Revolutions*; and Eric Davis, *Challenging Colonialism: Bank Misr and Egyptian Industrialization, 1920-1941*. They, at any rate, were the inspiration for both Joel Beinin and Zachary Lockman's *Workers on the Nile: Nationalism, Communism, Islam, and the Egyptian Working Class, 1882-1954* and Robert Vitalis's *When Capitalists Collide: Business Conflict and the End of Empire in Egypt*. Judith Tucker's *Women in Nineteenth-Century Egypt* and Kenneth Cuno's *The Pasha's Peasants: Land, Society, and Economy in Lower Egypt, 1740-1858* offered convincing refutations of the then dominant modernization theory understandings of the origins of capitalism and modernity in the Middle East. Those same questions were subsequently addressed in the Palestinian context by Beshara Doumani in *Rediscovering Palestine: Merchants and Peasants in Jabal Nablus, 1700-1900* and for Iraq by Dina Rizq Khoury in *State and Provincial Society in the Ottoman Empire: Mosul, 1540-1834*. Several political economy studies endeavored to understand the roots of Lebanon's implosion during the 1975-90 civil war, including Roger Owen (ed.), *Essays on the Crisis in Lebanon* and Akram Khater, *Inventing Home: Emigration, Gender, and the Middle Class in Lebanon, 1870-1920*. Owen's *The Middle East and the World Economy* and Roger Owen and Şevket Pamuk, *A History of Middle East Economies in the Twentieth Century*, while eschewing an explicit theoretical framework, offered a solid empirical ground for political economy studies, while Huri Islamoğlu-Inan (ed.) *The Ottoman Empire and the World Economy* usefully summarized and critiqued dependency theory approaches to the Middle East. Other texts are mentioned in my *Workers and Peasants in the Modern Middle East*. So from a historian's point of view, there are indeed foundational texts for the study of Middle East political economy.

Why did that intellectual tradition decline in the mid-1990s? Part of the reason is the "cultural turn" that affected historical studies and to a lesser extent other social sciences. A particular reason within the framework of Middle East studies is the enormous impact of Edward Said's *Orientalism*. It directed many cohorts of graduate students to the study of texts and representation rather than society. Said, unlike the postmodernists, did not believe that society does not exist. On the contrary he explicitly praised Anouar Abdel Malek, Samir Amin, Maxime Rodinson, Roger Owen, Abdullah Laraoui, Jacques Berque, and others who rejected culturalism. However, Said was a genius, despite his flaws. Very few scholars can keep as many intellectual balls in the air as he could. So the status of *Orientalism* as the best-known text of Middle East studies both in and outside the field has been an impediment to the development of political economy.

This need not be the case; it also offers an opportunity. None of the authors of these essays accepts the teleology and the "base/superstructure" model of Marx's formulations in the *Preface to a Contribution to the Critique of Political Economy*. We have learned that culture matters. Political economy studies should attempt to explain how it matters without reducing everything to it. This is an element of the intellectual agenda proposed in the Political Economy Project, or PEP, foundational statement:

> Political economy addresses the mutual constitution of states, markets, and classes, the co-constitution of class, race, gender, and other forms of identity, varying modes of capital accumulation and the legal, political, and cultural forms of their regulation, relations among local, national, and global forms of capital, class, and culture, the construction of forms of knowledge and hegemony; techno-politics; water and the environment as resources and fields of contestation; the role of war in the constitution of states and classes; and practices and cultures of domination and resistance.

[See page 13 for a complete list of participants in the Founding Workshop of the Political Economy Project, some of whose presentations are referenced in this introduction, but not included in the volume.]

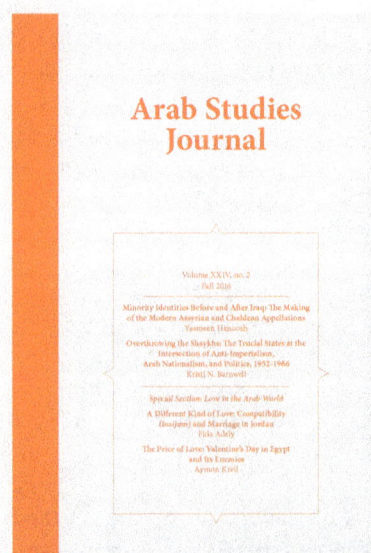

The Political Economy of Definition

Bassam Haddad The task of defining political economy is tricky, especially in a context where critical thinking drives the process, for the phrase itself offers its own problems, and that is only the starting point. Some caveats might help avoid pitfalls in trying to come together to build a network of researchers interested in the topic.

First, we are explicitly interested in a *critical* "political economy," not just the conception that refers ostensibly to the relationship between politics and economics. This sets one group of so-called political economists apart from another, or from others. The second caveat is that the phrase/term itself, as well as various definitions of it, can be replete with concepts and notions that are immediately contested, not least because they represent, in part, a liberal trajectory of writers and concerns—hence the importance of stressing "critical."

However, while these concerns are valid from one/our point of view, if we problematize endlessly, we become paralyzed, and if we do not problematize notions that contribute to the *re*production of existing social relations and means/modes of exploitation and disempowerment, we end up reproducing the social orders we inhabit.

Finally, I would like us not to assume simply that the discourse out there is problematic, and, if we use and promote a political economy approach, things might get better automatically. For sure, we are launching a project to do just that at some level, but I am also interested in us learning from each other as a community, challenging each other, and recognizing that having the right tool is only a starting point. The rest depends on what we do with it. I am not referring only to things that we have not studied or ventured into sufficiently, but to the very things and terms we assume, take for granted, and sometimes over-determine. Class is a good example. The notion of exploitation itself is another, and to combine these, the tension between anti-imperialism and a concern with class exploitation, is yet another. The Syrian situation is perhaps the most fitting case in point, and perhaps the one contemporary issue (definitely in the region) that has pitted people on the left against one another at various levels of intensity and animosity.

In sum, a critical political economy approach must heed its own advice and uphold reflexive and critical thinking at every turn. This is more of a challenge than it seems to be upon initial consideration.

My Own Work

In my initial work/research, I have invested a lot of time in debunking existing models of development that focused on liberal and neoliberal assumptions and prescriptions. I wrote, and write, about the political economy of authoritarian resilience for a variety of reasons that we continue to contend with today.

1. First, to provide an alternative non-culturalist explanation or narrative for the existence and persistence of authoritarianism. Political economy becomes at once a force that debunks and builds: it debunks stale cultural approaches and unimaginative, not to mention predetermined, political science mainstream concerns with "authority" and "patrimonialism." It also builds an alternative robust framework that explains both the prolonging of authoritarian rule at the macro level and the mechanics through which this takes place, the "how," at the micro-level that operates at the level of individuals and groups. Structure and agency thus have an explanatory place, but the direction of causality emanating from structural variables is always thicker.

2. Second, to identify the strong affinity between neoliberal prescriptions and the ruling classes—even in the case of Syria, which claimed to be socialist. I reveal the reasons why, in the case of a country that has refused to deal with international financial institutions like the World Bank and the International Monetary Fund, elites nonetheless adopted the same neoliberal prescriptions, because, by the 1980s and 1990s, these prescriptions conformed to both the class and political interests of these very elites, with rural and lower-middle class origins. This process perfected the notion of how politics and economics are always already fused, and the notion that they are separate comes primarily from language, not practice.

3. I also emphasized the political mediation and construction of class (i.e., the importance of processes through which political elites speed up and alter class structures over short periods of time, through ordinary tools we are familiar with, but also through networks, which can be alternative forms of conceptualizing agency). Over and above state-centered and society-centered approaches that do not explain adequately the existing and unfolding outcomes, the consolidation of class interests of political elites is expressed through public/private networks of capital that represent an alternative agency. This new form of agency, which is itself a vehicle for stimulating capital accumulation, class consciousness, and class consolidation, best explains contradictory outcomes that benefit neither the institutions of the state nor the amorphous conception of the "business community." Such political mediation created new social strata that came to be part of the long-term dominant class in Syria in less than two decades, and continued to prosper well into the 2000s. Such ascendance and its socio-economic consequences helped us understand both the growing resentment and later mobilization in Syria (starting, for good reason, in the countryside), and it helped us understand, in part, the stalling of the uprising in metropolitan cities.

4. The last point that I sought to debunk or correct from a critical perspective is that ubiquitously used and misplaced notion of corruption (i.e., that problems in the regional economic landscape emanate from corruption in the context of authoritarian rule). This is a formidable liberal and neoliberal trope

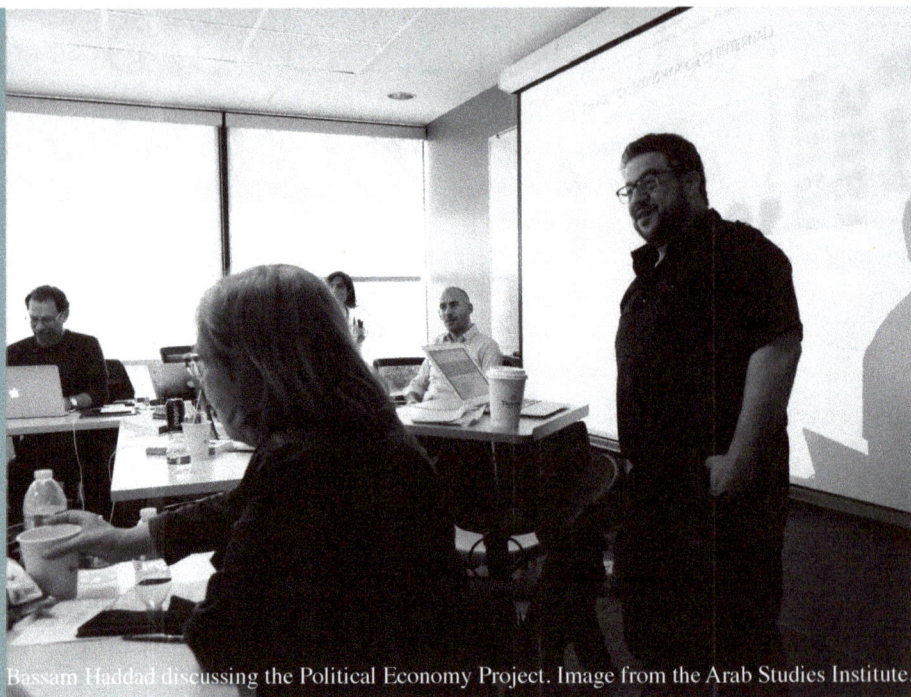

> *Beyond all the pontifications and differences, it can be considered a victory of sorts if we are able to tilt the explanatory cannons away from essentially culturalist explanations and toward ones dealing with political economy, notwithstanding that the latter is not infallible.*

Bassam Haddad discussing the Political Economy Project. Image from the Arab Studies Institute.

that denies what Aref Dalila, the Syrian economist, called the material base of corruption, and associated it with dynamics of class and capital that are only facilitated by authoritarian rule, not created by it. This observation paved the way to addressing how that trope of so-called corruption, or, in effect, class exploitation, travels well and applies just as much to the United States, except it proceeds legally for the most part and is interrupted only infrequently when a constellation of factors makes such practices impermissible.

My current research applies this and other frameworks to a much broader period that extends from the 1930s-1940s to 2011 in Syria. I move away from debunking myths and correcting explanatory faux-pas, and into articulating an argument about slow moving socioeconomic and sociopolitical factors that animate more than seventy years of Syria's history. In this research, I highlight the structural and structuring power of capital in altering political rationalities to suit capital accumulation in a society and an economy with poorly consolidated class interests, giving way to intermediary concepts such as networks. I borrow from the classic cannons of political economy as well as innovative economic sociology, with a fortunate dose of access to actual records from Syria.

"What Is To Be Done?" It Is Not As Simple As Sticking to Good Principles/Ideas

My politico-analytical take away is to recognize that there is no substitution for political work and, thus, collective action, both theoretically and practically. We may differ as to how to proceed intellectually/theoretically. Some advocate reform. I personally do not feel that this is what is needed, discursively or practically. Reform might beautify or mend temporarily, but, whereas most, if not all of us opine that it is not enough to reform, it also may not possible to overhaul, according to a rushed timetable. Therefore, at the collective action level, the question remains: what is to be done in the mean time?

Broadly speaking, I urge us to think of matters not just in terms of what they are, but in terms of how they can be shaped, without losing sight of some core guiding principles. These are: analyzing, challenging, deconstructing, supplanting, and unraveling mechanisms of exploitation and disempowerment in reference to sociopolitical, socioeconomic, gender-, sexuality-, ethnic-, racial-based, and, yes, environmental matters—that detail that seems to be parasitic instead of being a core component of critical analysis. I would like us to recognize our strongest common denominators, and build on those, because, with time, we will all be surprised how such movement will allow us to grow, individually and as a collective. Given we do not radically differ on basic principles, temperament is crucial to smooth and productive operations and, ultimately, impact.

Intellectual Starting Points: The Explanatory Factor and the Real World

I would like for this project to advance the use and utility of political economy as an analytical tool for explanatory purposes. Beyond all the pontifications and differences, it can be considered a victory of sorts if we are able to tilt the explanatory cannons away from essentially culturalist explanations and toward ones dealing with political economy, notwithstanding that the latter is not infallible. That is only a starting point.

I, as well as my colleague Hanieh, see several avenues that stem from our initial conception of this project, all of which can only be enriched by discussion. These items are part of what propelled the initiation of this project:

1. To approximate such a state of affairs regarding the explanatory weight of political economy approaches, we must encourage political economy-related research and production among researchers and political economy works among readers, while creating new categories of researchers and readers. Bringing critical political economy into the center of discussion, rather than having it be in the often marginalized back seat (called upon as an afterthought), is a good target for this project.

2. There is perhaps no better or more efficient way given our means and positionality than to target the pedagogical realm for this purpose. Providing pedagogical tools dealing with political economy for educators at all levels is key to reviving, introducing, or strengthening instruction in this direction. This can take place in a variety of ways that no one treatise can exhaust. It could include curating reading materials, providing instruction modules, and preparing a variety of useful resources on a portal that will eventually be known to many educators, including those of us participating in its production. We should not assume that only others can learn from what we can produce as a collective.

3. To do so, and to do much more, this project will benefit immensely from the development of a network, or a community of researchers, educators, journalists, and writers who share an interest in advancing the study of political economy. The development of such a community is crucial if we are to have some impact on research, pedagogy, and, potentially, stakeholders struggling for rights or against mechanisms of exploitation. Furthermore, this community can become an incubator of sorts for various initiatives that cannot be determined in advance. One of the most important aspects of this project is that it is, and should be, cross-regional, and not centered solely on the Middle East. Though this will take some time to materialize, it is through the community/networks that we can realize this extension and benefit from other experiences/ paradigms—and vice versa. Much more can be said about this aspect of the project, but it is best for such ideas to proceed organically through engagement and discussion.

4. A fourth and less pronounced aspect that can benefit this project, is the production of outreach campaigns and messaging (using old and new social media and beyond). If we are to target all demographics, such approaches can trigger and mobilize often just as much, if not more, than really well-thought out and researched literature—unfortunately. The trick here is to be strategic and maintain the right balance between substance and instrumentality. Moreover, this project can lend a hand to such endeavors and not necessarily participate in them. Thus, a consultancy role can be on the cards naturally as we are approached by individuals and organizations seeking our input.

5. More along the above lines, but far more organic, is the last suggested dimension that Hanieh and I, among many others, feel strongly about as this project moves forward: we see that this project can, with time, establish a bridge between what we can provide as a community/network and actual like-minded groups on the ground in the region, but also beyond. The provision of legal and intellectual support and connection with stakeholders working on social justice enhances the impact of the project and prevents a descent into an ivory-tower affair. This can proceed at various levels, the feasibility and utility of which can be discussed collectively. Again, we can also act as facilitators in this regard, not just as participants. In all cases, I do not think that we will lose sight of what we can do best—i.e., there is little to no risk of getting overstretched or overcommitted given our existing commitments as individuals. However, given that there is no pre-condition that network members be "scholars," such a connection is not far-fetched.

POLITICAL ECONOMY PROJECT
SUMMER INSTITUTE

Over the course of four days, 9-12 June 2016, and in conjunction with ASI and Arcadia University, the Political Economy Project held its inaugural Political Economy Summer Institute (PESI) at George Mason University. The summer institute brought together a diverse collection of scholars and graduate student fellows from around the world for a series of workshops on the foundational concerns of critical political economy, with special attention devoted to conducting research in the contemporary Middle East. The institute served not only as an overview of critical debates and fundamental concepts for student participants, but also as an opportunity for faculty participants to reflect on long-running debates and acquaint themselves with emerging research agendas.

More information is available at:
www.politicaleconomyproject.org/summer-institute.html

Spaces of Political Economy

Adam Hanieh

What I understand by "political economy" encapsulates a wide range of perspectives aimed at understanding the contemporary configuration of social power and the ways it has developed historically. This includes, of course, mainstream neoclassical and institutionalist political economy, as well as more critical approaches. I situate my own work within a Marxian framework, with the understanding that there is no single "correct" Marxist approach, but a variety of insights and debates that must be continually developed through interaction with concrete reality. To my mind, the strength of Marxism lies in (1) the insistence on the conflictual, exploitative, and contradictory nature of capitalist development; (2) an emphasis on mapping social relations and their institutional forms; and (3) a focus on a social totality that encompasses not only distributional patterns and institutions, but also the exploitative nature of the capital-labor relation.

My specific country-based research on the region has tended to focus upon on the Gulf Arab states and on Palestine. However, within this, I have tried to pursue a regional approach that situates these areas within the development of capitalism at a regional scale and within the world market. More generally, I am interested in how relations of class form and continue to change in the Arab world. Who constitutes the capitalist classes in the Arab world? How did these classes originate, and how is their accumulation structured? How is the formation of labor connected to the dominance of capital? How do political forms and institutions–such as the state and the military–mediate these relationships of power? And, particularly importantly, how are these relationships located within the wider global political economy, as well as through regional linkages?

> *The connection between the political and the economic is particularly important to emphasize today, as it points to the necessary linkage between the struggle to address socioeconomic inequalities and those aimed at political reform.*

In pursuing these questions, there are three key themes that I constantly find myself grappling with:

1. **The relationship between politics and economics.** To a degree I do not particularly like the term "political economy," as I think it tends to reinforce a division between politics and economics as separate spheres that may interact but can also stand distinct from one another. We can see this today in many of the contemporary political debates in the Middle East, where much of the focus has been on attempts to build liberal democratic structures and new constitutional models, while keeping in place the same types of economic policies that preceded 2011 and 2012. This approach sees liberalized markets as apolitical and separate from the question of political power.

In contrast, I would agree with the numerous scholars who argue that we need to see the political and economic spheres as fused: political forms reflect and mediate economic power. The connection between the political and the economic is particularly important to emphasize today, as it points to the necessary linkage between the struggle to address socioeconomic inequalities and those aimed at political reform.

2. **The ways in which different spatial scales are related across the world market.** One of the things I try to do in my own research is work against the prevailing "methodological nationalism" that I think typifies a lot of the dominant ways of thinking about the Middle East. In other words, we need to be cognizant of how nation states are not neatly bounded sets of social relations, but are always tied to regional and global processes. This has important implications for how we think of class and state formation in the Middle East, and a lot of my own work has been focused on looking at how we can understand the political economy of the Middle East through a regional lens (and as part of the world market). At a methodological level, I think there is much we can learn about these questions through examining other historical processes. For this reason, I have been reading a lot recently on the histories of sugar, slavery, cotton, and the development of capitalism and the world market. I find this literature very interesting because it really grapples with the ways that we need to think of the emergence of capitalism as a global process, with a constant reshaping of relationships between national (and sub-national) processes.

3. Running through both these questions is **how we think of categories such as class and state, and their interaction with other social categories such as gender, race, nationality, and so forth.** Here I draw inspiration from the work of Bertell Ollman, particularly his concept of "internal relations," which emphasizes the mutually constructed nature of all analytical categories. The focus here is placed on understanding reality as composed of relations rather than independent, discrete phenomena. I believe this approach helps us avoid an abstract and economistic understanding of what we mean, for example, by class. Questions such as gender, age, national and ethnic origin, citizenship status, and so forth, are part of what constitutes class as a concrete social relation. In this sense, class is not an abstract category shorn of particularity and difference—difference is essential to how we understand it. As David McNally has recently noted, drawing upon the insights of the Canadian theorist Himani Bannerji, we need to avoid an approach that sees "different forms of social oppression as discrete and autonomous social relations ... rather than as 'social relations and forms [that] come into being in and through each other.'"[1] From this perspective, the emphasis is placed on understanding how these relations exist and change, and, most significantly, on understanding these relations as part of

what actually constitutes the categories (such as class) through which we can view the world.

This means, for example, that it makes little sense to speak of class without also acknowledging that it is simultaneously gendered as it forms. This gendering process is part of what class is—the latter concept cannot be fully understood without incorporating this relationship into its theorization.[2] Class in the Arab world, for example, is gendered in a very particular way—the marginalization of women within labor force participation,

The Political Economy Project Founding Workshop at George Mason University. Image from the Arab Studies Institute.

the exclusion of female university graduates, the feminization of certain types of labor (e.g., garment sectors in Morocco and Tunisia, agriculture in much of the region), and so forth. It also involves a range of different types of labor relationships (seen, perhaps most importantly, in the informal sector). Class is also constituted through the profound movements of people across and within borders—it is thus marked by differences around status and citizenship. In all of these cases, an appreciation of these internal relations is essential to understanding what constitutes class.

What do I hope to see come out of the Political Economy Project? First, I think it would be enormously useful to build a network of critical scholars working on different aspects of the political economy of the Middle East. I believe that we remain much too divided along country specialization and disciplinary interests, and that encouraging a process through which we can engage with one another around broader methodological themes could be very stimulating. Furthermore, having completed my PhD in Canada but working now for several years in the United Kingdom, I feel there is a relative lack of cross-engagement between North American and European scholars working on Middle East political economy (let alone those from the region itself!). I think building these pan-continental links could also be very enriching.

I also feel that we need to better engage with debates occurring in political economy outside of a strictly Middle East focus. There has been quite a resurgence of critical political economy in recent years, particularly since the onset of the global economic crisis, and I firmly believe we need to integrate these debates into how we understand regional processes. This is not just true at a general theoretical level; I think we need much more exposure to how schol-

ars are tackling questions of understanding capitalism in places such as East Asia and Latin America.

The final point I would make is the necessity of utilizing any political economy network to assist and build solidarity with social movements in the region itself. To my mind this is actually the most exciting aspect of this project. I think there is a plethora of new movements and intellectual currents that have developed across the region over recent years, and yet we often respond to these in an individual capacity or through limited forms of political engagement that are seen as separate from our academic interests. I am excited to see how we can build upon our links to help assist these movements on the ground.

Endnotes:

1. David McNally, "The dialectics of unity and difference in the constitution of wage-labour: On internal relations and working-class formation," *Capital & Class* 39, no. 1 (2015), 131–146, 143.

2. Ibid. To be clear, this argument is not meant to reduce categories such as gender, national origin, and so forth to simply class relations. In the article cited, McNally comments: "there is no social relation of, say, race, that is not internally related to sexuality, gender and class, and therefore constituted in and through these relations. To be sure, these different social forms can be analytically distinguished, just as they are distinguished in experience; but this should not entail the error of imagining that they actually exist as discrete 'things,' which then enter into external contact with each other."

A Political Economy to Call Our Own

Shana Marshall   As an explanatory framework, political economy has certainly increased its stature among Middle East scholars, not least due to the events of the Arab Spring, but if one were to search for the professional and pedagogical indicators of a thriving subfield of Middle East political economy, many would be absent. The nature and features of this absence may tell us a great deal about the discipline and the politics of the questions we study.

First, what are the indicators of a subfield's coherence and/or institutionalization? Is it a canonical set of texts; a flagship journal; a widely recognized and replicated vocabulary; graduate courses; university-endowed chairs; postdoctoral fellowships? Unlike the political economy of other regions (Latin America, East Asia, Sub-Saharan Africa), Middle East political economy hardly satisfies any of these criteria. What most would consider the English-language flagship journal of the subfield, *The Middle East Report*, while an excellent example of scholarship and informed analysis, is published by a non-profit organization and is not technically peer reviewed and therefore does not count for tenure or promotion. Other publications that served this purpose in the past have ceased to perform that function. The *Review of Middle East Studies* is more of an organizational bulletin than a journal, and *Arab Studies Quarterly* does not explicitly focus on political economy scholarship. This is not the case with other area studies subfields, which have their own explicitly political-economy oriented publications: such as *Review of African Political Economy*; *Latin American Perspectives*; *European Journal of Political Economy*; *Post Communist Economies*; and the *Journal of Economic Perspectives* (North America and Western Europe).

There is really only one work that would qualify as a basic instructional/reference text–Richards and Waterbury's *A Political Economy of the Middle East*—and it was originally published in 1992, with only modest updates to subsequent editions. (Only in the wake of the Arab Spring—and the widespread calls for bread and social justice—has a substantively new edition been commissioned, co-authored by Ishac Diwan and fellow PEP member Melani Cammet). There are no endowed chairs (as far as I know) in Middle East political economy, no university press publishes a series in "Middle East political economy"—though again, such series exist for other regions—nor is there (to my knowledge) a postdoctoral fellowship for Middle East political economy. Of the handful of academic texts that appear on virtually every regional political economy syllabus, few were written after 1999. Many are economic histories or single case studies, which, although of immense value, do not explicitly link up to broader systemic questions relating to the region's role in the global economy or compare the patterns and dynamics of the region's domestic economies. (I am not speaking here of mainstream political economy syllabi, which are primarily comprised of technical reports from international financial institutions and studies of econometric models that bear no resemblance to actual economies).

Why are so many of these subfield features absent? Unlike many vibrant and productive (also newer and more esoteric) fields like ethnomusicology, political economy did not "branch off" from a pre-existing field of study after decades of increased specialization by practitioners. In the beginning, political economy was "all of" politics and very nearly "all of" social science. Today, many academic departments do not even maintain political economy as a stand-alone subfield. The American Political Science Association has relegated it to one of forty-three "organized sections," alongside such specialized fields of study as "health policy" and "sexuality and politics."

> *Is it the scholarly consensus that Middle East political economy exists only as a marginal subfield? Or, conversely, is it the case that political-economic research questions are so ubiquitous that very little research actually falls outside the practical boundary of the discipline?*

I must confess I have no formal training in political economy. The survey course was not offered during my time as a PhD student (an indicator of the field's lack of importance in the view of university leadership, a trend present in many institutions, as noted in fellow PEP member Omar Dahi's essay). I came to political economy because I saw it as the best method of analysis for examining the power and influence of militaries in the Middle East, which was my main institution of interest. I quickly realized that in order to understand the enclave economies operated by the region's armed forces—which are increasingly active participants in the institutions of global capitalism—I needed an understanding of contemporary financial markets, corporate economics and private equity markets, to name just a few. As many regional militaries are partnering with transnational firms and domestic private sector elites to expand their operations in the era of shrinking public sector budgets, it is the institutions and relationships of the contemporary capitalist economy that are central to military power and influence.

In 1996 Bob Vitalis lamented "the decline of political economy as a productive mode of intellectual inquiry by students of the Middle East." This was partly due to the decline of dependency theory explanations more broadly (and so the decline of political economy in general), but also due to the fact that its Middle East manifestation was largely derivative of the theories and concepts developed by political economists studying other third world regions, and so had no foundation to return to once dependency theory ceased to drive scholarly inquiry.

One possible explanation for this derivative quality is the high degree of colonial penetration in the Middle East. Where indigenous economies remained intact, these became a subject for economic historians and economic anthropologists (not political economists), and where they were thoroughly integrated into the global economy, through war-time supply chains, foreign oil and gas companies, and other transnational actors, they were taken up by international relations theorists. Thus there was no real "Middle East political economy" to call our own. The unique areas of inquiry—such as peasant studies—that produced enormous research agendas in other regions were not nearly so productive in Middle East area studies. Some of this is for obvious reasons: large parts of the region are unsuitable for agriculture, and the relatively low population density probably made for less organized rural political actions (and therefore less research attention). The exception would be Egypt, which, unlike the rest of the region, had large agrarian populations similar to those in Asia (and was also the subject of serious inquiry within the field of peasant studies), but even regions with relatively smaller populations (such as Eastern Europe and Latin America) and arid landscapes (the Sahel) still figure prominently in contemporary peasant studies literature, while the Arab Middle East does not. Since peasant studies was a large part of political economy in the 1970s and 1980s, perhaps a great number of graduate students interested in these questions migrated away from Middle East studies (or away from political economy). Hence, today we have comparatively fewer scholars trained explicitly in the political economy of the Middle East.

Is it the scholarly consensus that Middle East political economy exists only as a marginal subfield? Or, conversely, is it the case that political-economic research questions are so ubiquitous that very little research actually falls *outside* the practical boundary of the discipline? A better set of questions then might be, what research questions or research agendas *do not* make use of theories and concepts that have grown out of the study of political economy? Is putting up signposts with a specialized vocabulary to say "this is political economy" unnecessary for Middle East scholars? And, if so, why has this not been the case in other area studies political economy fields? What is lost when scholars do not employ the explicit vocabulary of political economy, specifically for training of graduate students but also for attracting resources for workshops, conferences, graduate courses, working groups, fellowships, etc.? Are other area studies regions characterized by the same disaggregation (or disintegration) of their political-economy subfields?

I would argue that much is lost when our research is not explicit in its orientation toward political economy—and that much must be done to revive the approach, especially in the United States, through cultivating pedagogical and professional resources. No scholar with even a passing knowledge of contemporary popular thought or disciplinary history would suggest that the political economy approach has been victorious in its battle with neoclassical economics. An economics dictionary from 1913 reads "although the name political economy is still preserved, the science, as now understood, is not strictly political: i.e., it is not confined to relations between the government and the governed, but deals primarily with the industrial activities of individual men." Clearly this definition applies to the contemporary discipline of economics–specifically research that utilizes econometric methods. What field then is responsible for studying relations between the government and the governed when these relations are primarily influenced by extreme asymmetries in the possession and accumulation of economic power (capital)? Despite the painfully obvious truth that capital clearly dictates political outcomes in even the most procedurally democratic contexts, the subfield best suited to examining and explaining this relationship (political economy) is being pushed to the margins. The imperative to revive it in the context of Middle East area studies is as pressing now as ever.

POLITICAL ECONOMY PROJECT

Founding Workshop, April 2015

Founded by the Arab Studies Institute
Co-sponsored with Middle East and Islamic Studies at GMU

CO-FOUNDERS
Bassam Haddad
Adam Hanieh

PARTICIPANTS
Bassam Haddad
Adam Hanieh
Sherene Seikaly
Omar Dahi
Ziad Abu-Rish
Joel Beinin
Toby Jones
Melani Cammett
Laleh Khalili
Max Ajl
Pete Moore
Ahmad Shokr
Paul Amar
Aaron Jakes
Wael Gamal
Rafeef Ziadah
Charles Anderson
Firat Bozcali
Toufic Haddad
Mandy Turner
Shana Marshall
John Warner

Jadaliyya جدليّة

JADMAG PEDAGOGY PUBLICATIONS ISSUE 4.2

Beyond Fayyadism: The Historical Tools of Political Economy

Sherene Seikaly In exploring the inextricable links between governance, calculability, scarcity, and basic needs during World War II, I was struck time and again by the resonance between the government policies that sought to contain the poor in Britain and the colonized in Palestine.[1] Indeed, the figure of the impoverished and the colonized took shape as differentiated but parallel objects of fear, despise, and potential reform. Political economy is a set of tools that allows me to trace this resonance not as coincidental or anomalous, but as structural and formative of the technologies of rule.

In my own work, I have used political economy to think about how colonialism is a form of enterprise and how this perspective can shed new light on the question of Israel/Palestine. The creation of the kibbutz in early twentieth-century Palestine was not only a form of identity and land settlement, it was also a form of economic enterprise linked to nineteenth-century socialism. This enterprise created a new ethical opportunity to produce goods and subjectivities. But where is the Palestinian part of this economic story?

In economic narratives, Palestinians before 1948 take shape as nameless, dispossessed peasants; members of a small but heroic number of workers; and a staid group of reactionary elites. Labor historians, as well as scholars of subaltern studies more broadly, have detailed a landscape of strategies, experiences, and discourses that have complicated this nameless peasant and the seemingly irrelevant worker,[2] but the businessman remains invisible. The question I posed in in this context was what do we do with the historically constituted and significant commercial class in Palestine?

Typically it is difficult to access these people or make sense of their projects because their position as bourgeois renders them both easily understood and politically suspect. They are time and again failed actors; they cannot be significant nor part of the shaping of national or regional transformations and imaginings.

However, taking these actors seriously helps us make a number of crucial turns. One, these actors help us question normative understandings of capitalism. Here it is crucial to heed the lessons of the feminist geographers Julie Graham and Katherine Gibson. Gibson and Graham cautioned against repeating a narrative of capitalism, which can unwittingly reinforce its power as an ideologically coherent and singular agent rather than a process.[3] Inspired by an anthropology of concepts in the sphere of the economic, I headed these lessons by turning to the language and concepts of the time to mine political and economic struggles, debates, and strategies.

This was easiest to trace in the sphere of consumption where my work began. There was a deep debate on the ethics of consumption among Palestinians and in particular their relationship to saving and spending money. I was able to begin further exploring both production and consumption and their relationship to ethics. Here the literature on luxury within moral philosophy, before the turn to political economy, was crucial. Istavan Hont's work on Adam Smith, and his writing on luxury, have been enlightening in this regard.[4] This work is crucial for two reasons. One, Smith was one of the most widely read and cited source among the Palestinians I studied. Two, returning critically to these texts helps us rethink the salient right wing appropriation of Smith that has become conventional wisdom, at least in university curricula on economic thought.

So what did these actors actually do in Palestine in the early twentieth century? Palestinian merchants, businessmen, and economic thinkers drew on a rich discursive and political world in their efforts to make money and nation. This included and fed into the broader nineteenth-century project of the *nahda* and also drew a longer trajectory of theories of saving and spending. They also adapted and drew on centuries of experience of long distance trade and property forms. Their world was a complicated one that cannot make sense if we attempt to use ready-made terms to understand it.

> In order to envision the future, we have to better understand the political and economic debates that have shaped our political imagination in the present. In the case of Palestinian economic thought, we can no longer afford to begin such a history in 1948.

Why do these actors matter? My aim was to trace a historical trajectory that engaged Fayyadism, as the Palestinian's embrace of neoliberalism is widely referred to, inspired by the figure of the Palestinian Authority's former prime minister, Salam Fayyad. I wanted to show that the investment in private property, capital accumulation, and self-responsibility did not begin in 1967, or 1948, as most contemporary accounts of Palestinian economic thought and practice presently contend.[5]

My project was not an attempt to recover a heroic and silenced agent of productivity and profit accumulation. However, the impulse to recover became harder to resist when I confronted time and again, a resilient and pervasive insistence among scholars and everyday people, both in Palestine and outside of it, that there was no commercial or middle class before 1948. If it did exist, many insisted, it was so failed and so clearly an agent of colonial power that it was irresponsible to even bother studying it. Thus, time and again these particular elites were either invisible or so staid that they did not innovate new forms of capital accumulation and politics.

However, these conclusions were hard to square with the post 1948 reality. Indeed, the small group of men I studied, including Fu'ad

Sherene Seikaly at the PEP Founding Workshop. Image from the Arab Studies Institute.

yachar also warns against turning neoliberalism from a process into an epithet. This insight has pushed me in my own work to explore the terms and ideas that Palestinian elites shaped and innovated and to resist using ready-made terms to describe a set of practices, priorities, and visions that are hard to comprehend in today's world.[8] In fact, this is why, at Elyachar's insistence, I began calling what my historical subjects called themselves, men of capital, as opposed to what I had been calling them: capitalists.

What can this past tell us about the present? By looking careful at men, and to a lesser extent, women of capital in twentieth-century Palestine, we can find some of the lasting legacies that shape our present. First, the formation of class and status did not simply seek to reinforce existing hierarchies but sought to create new ones. Second, the formation of a national economy had its roots in regional imaginings of free trade and capitalist utopia. Third, economic thought and the imperative of capital accumulation were central to the Arab liberal project, or the *nahda*. The *nahda* was not then only cultural or literary, it was also economic. In Palestine, and beyond, we need to shift our thinking so that we can account for an Arab liberal project that has its foundational roots in capital accumulation and private property. Fourth, the work of making economy, both nationally and regionally, was inextricable from the shaping of a separate and parallel domestic space. The home was a site of moral, economic, and social regulation and containment. In these interlocking and parallel spaces, there are a number of gendered norms that inform the present. One notable point here is the idea that a woman is responsible for guarding her man's fidelity, and protecting him from his natural tendency to spend, by keeping a clean, simply, rationally managed home.

To conclude, I will return here to some reflections on political economy and what it makes possible. I have been inspired by Aaron Jakes' powerful invitation not to treat economic life as an unchanging landscape to whatever story is at hand.[9] Taking this invitation seriously would make it impossible to render, as recent scholarship has done, Arab economy as simply a shadow of a Jewish economy in British-ruled Palestine.[10]

A return to political economy forces us to explore and challenge how material conditions are connected to disciplinary and knowledge formations.

Here I want to end with a point about neoliberalism and its relationship to knowledge production and higher education more broadly. One is about the cultural turn itself. Chris Hann and Keith Hart have connected the cultural turn to neoliberal dominance beginning in the 1980s. They suggest that the defeat of organized labor as well as market infiltration of public and domestic life was responsible in part for the scholarly emphasis on meaning and subjectivity.[11] However, I want to caution here

Saba, Abd al-Muhsin al-Qattan, Ahmad Hilmi Pasha, among others would become leading figures in accounting, banking, and insurance throughout the Arab world after 1948. They had before 1948 established ventures that would go on to wield extensive financial power on a regional scale. These ventures included the Arab Bank, Arabia Insurance Company, and Saba and Company. In the 1930s and 1940s, in various forums such as the Chambers of Commerce, and the periodical *Al-Iqtisadiyyat al-'Arabiyya*, Palestinian economic thinkers shaped the horizon of a regional capitalist utopia.

I would like to return here to the insistence that the commercial, and small but growing industrial class, was at once so insignificant and so politically abhorrent as to be undeserving of study. This perspective speaks to more than the specific question of Palestine. It reflects a contemporary pattern of political analysis. For too long, both radical and conservative scholars across disciplinary divides have understood right leaning policies and practices as unchanging. We should at this point know better. The right across geographic and temporal borders is an innovative force. Closely linked to this understanding of the right wing as staid is our use of neoliberalism as a way to say everything and nothing at once. Here, I have been particularly inspired by Paul Amar's mapping of what he calls the "heuristic device" of the human-security state to trouble the staid authoritarian and the ever-illusive neoliberal.[6]

I also take my cue from Julia Elyachar's reflections on tacit knowledge and neoliberalism in two ways.[7] First, as she suggests, in order to envision the future, we have to better understand the political and economic debates that have shaped our political imagination in the present. In the case of Palestinian economic thought, we can no longer afford to begin such a history in 1948. Second, El-

against throwing the lessons of the cultural turn into the wastebasket of failed ivory tower musings.[12] To dispense with the lessons of scholars like Judith Butler, Franz Fanon, Gayatri Spivak, and Edward Said, would hinder our engagement with race, gender, sex, and class as lived material experiences and constructs. It would disable our capacity to do what political economy empowers us to do: not simply to analyze inequality but to confront, contest, and challenge it.

Endnotes:

1. See Sherene Seikaly, *Men of Capital: Scarcity and Economy in Mandate Palestine* (Stanford: Stanford University Press, 2016).

2. Charles Anderson, "From Petition to Confrontation: the Palestinian National Movement and the Rise of Mass Politics, 1929-1939," PhD dissertation (New York University, 2013); Joel Beinin, *Workers and Peasants in the Modern Middle East* (Cambridge: Cambridge University Press, 2001); Zachary Lockman, *Comrades and Enemies: Arab and Jewish Workers in Palestine, 1906-1948* (Berkeley: University of California Press, 1996).

3. J.K. Gibson-Graham

4. Istvan Hont and Michael Ignatieff, "Needs and Justice in the Wealth of Nations: An Introductory Essay," in Istvan Hont and Michael Ignatieff (eds.), *Wealth and Virtue: The Shaping of Political Economy in the Scottish Enlightenment* (Cambridge: Cambridge University Press, 1983); and Adam Smith, *An Inquiry into the Nature and Causes of the Wealth of Nations* R. H. Campbell and A. S. Skinner (eds.) (Oxford: Clarendon, 1976) [1795].

5. Raja Khalidi, "The Economics of Palestinian Liberation," *Jacobin*, 15 October 2014.

6. Paul Amar, *The Security Archipelago: Human-Security States, Sexuality Politics, and the End of Neoliberalism* (Duke University Press, 2013)

7. Julia Elyachar, "Before and After Neoliberalism: Tacit Knowledge, Secrets of the Trade, and the Public Sector in Egypt," *Cultural Anthropology* 27, no. 1 (2012): 76-96.

8. An example of what this approach could look like is Elyachar's reflection on the term *fahlawah*, which means cleverness, alertness, street smarts, trickery, and secrets of the trade. She discusses how the economist Talal Abdel-Malak uses *fahlawah* to describe how Hosni Mubarak's regime verbally complied with US and IMF orders to privatize, while maintaining practical resistance. Elyachar, "Before and After Neoliberalism," 86; Talaat Abdel-Malek, "Export: The Five Piece Puzzle." *Al-Ahram* Weekly 587, May 23-29. Elyachar uses *fahlawah* to think through the notion of tacit knowledge, which Polanyi and Hayek located in each individual. These individuals were woven together in the market into a broader whole, through a price system that translated tacit knowledge into useful experience. However, in Cairo, among workshop owners, she shows, the situation is different: information is not accessible through a uniform prices system, but rather, knowledge is transmitted across generations, through apprenticeship, and horizontally from the workshop to the street. Secrets of the trade were another form of tacit knowledge in the market among the craft workers and public sector bankers that Elyachar worked with. By uncovering these forms of knowledge and value, she does not simply question the ideological coherence of neoliberalism but attempts more importantly to see "traces of the future in the disasters that neoliberalism have wrought." (91)

9. Aaron Jakes, "Review Essay: A New Materialism? Globalization and Technology in the Age of Empire," *International Journal of Middle East Studies* 47, no. 2 (April 2015): 369-381.

10. Ronen Shamir, Current Flow: *The Electrification of Palestine* (Stanford: Stanford University Press, 2013).

11. Chris Hann and Keith Hart, *Economic Anthropology: History, Ethnography, Critique* (Cambridge: Polity Press, 2011), 86.

12. See here Vivek Chibber's *Postcolonial Theory and the Specter of Capital* (London: Verso, 2013); the confrontation between Chibber and Partha Chatterjee at the Historical Materialism Conference in New York, http://navayana.org/blog/2013/05/07/vivek-chibberpartha-chatterjee-face-off-2013/; Gayatri Spivak, "Postcolonial Theory and the Specter of Capital," *Cambridge Review of International Affairs* 27: 1 (2014); and Chibber, "Making Sense of Postcolonial Theory: a Response to Gayatri Chakravorty Spivak" in *Cambridge Review of International Affairs* 27: 3 (2014).

How Political Economy can Illuminate Important Questions

JADMAG PEDAGOGY PUBLICATIONS ISSUE 4.2

Melani Cammett A mainstream understanding in the discipline of political science treats political economy as an analytical approach involving the application of tools and concepts from economics to the study political phenomena. I view political economy differently, even if I think it can be useful to borrow from economics, among other disciplines, to study politics. I take political economy to be the intersection of politics and economics. In this interpretation, political economy involves studying how politics shape economic outcomes or, conversely, how economic factors shape politics. In my view, politics and economics intersect virtually everywhere: we cannot study economic phenomena without politics, and often (but not always) we cannot study politics without attention to economic factors. In short, political economy is fundamental to addressing core questions about "who gets what, when and how?"

I describe myself as a scholar who specializes in the political economy of development and the Middle East[1] and North Africa (MENA). My past, current, and new research projects, which largely focus on the Middle East, address a variety of related themes, including the politics of economic and social outcomes; the political economy of identity politics; and the interaction of politics and economics in shaping development trajectories. These projects range from relatively micro-level work centered on a single country or subnational units to broad, cross-national work covering the Middle East as a whole. Some of my work on political economy entails more abstract theory development applicable to post-colonial developing countries within and beyond the Middle East.

The Politics of Economic and Social Outcomes

Several of my current research projects focus on the ways in which certain dimensions of "governance," especially accountability and participation, affect the nature and quality of social provision. I recently completed a series of pilot surveys in Greater Beirut, Lebanon that assess the quality of primary health care at the facility level, with comparisons across health centers run by the public sector, secular NGOs, religious charities and political parties. I am currently scaling up this research to the national level and am working on a related project in Jordan, which focuses on how facility and community-level formal and informal mechanisms of accountability affect the quality of care, but only in public primary health centers. Finally, I am designing a set of experimental interventions to examine how elite and nonelite community participation affects the quality of primary health care in public health centers in rural Morocco.

My next major book project also examines the politics of economic and social outcomes but focuses on a different set of questions and uses distinct methods. In this project, I aim to examine the long-term historical roots of variation in development trajectories and social welfare regimes in the Middle East. The crux of the project centers on the effects of Ottoman and colonial-era institutional development on post-independence development in the region. This project was in part inspired by the spate of work on other regions addressing similar questions (for example, see the work of Daron Acemoglu and James Robinson, James Mahoney and Hillel Soifer) and in part a response to approaches that treat development in the Middle East and, more generally, the "Islamic world" in a monolithic fashion.

> In political science much research on the Middle East has focused on the roots of persistent authoritarianism or Islamism. While these are productive and important research agendas, they may have crowded out work on other topics, which may be more germane to the interests of people in the region.

The Political Economy of Identity Politics

A related area of research focuses on the ways in which sectarianism constitutes and is constituted by socioeconomic institutions and policies. Much of my scholarship in this vein has focused on Lebanon, which is a fruitful place to address these questions for obvious reasons. My current research, comparing the quality of social provision by religious charities, sectarian parties and politicians, and other types of providers, fits here. I am also in the early stages of designing two different collaborative research projects, which examine altruistic and prosocial behavior towards outgroup members as well as inter-group relations in the allocation of social goods. The impetus for these projects stems in part from research I conducted for my book, *Compassionate Communalism: Welfare and Sectarianism in Lebanon* (Cornell University Press, 2014), which explores the political motivations shaping the distribution of welfare goods by sectarian groups and from my co-edited volume (with Lauren Morris MacLean), *The Politics of Non-State Social Welfare* (Cornell University Press, 2014), which examines the political consequences of welfare supplied by a range of international and locally rooted non-state providers.

The Interaction Between Politics and Economics

A broad theme in some of my work emphasizes the interaction between politics and economics. My first book, *Globalization and Business Politics in North Africa* (Cambridge University Press, 2007, 2010), examined the varied ways in which Moroccan and Tunisian business groups responded to threats and opportunities from the global economy. Focusing on the same industrial sectors in the two countries, I aimed to show how distinct patterns of state-business relations and capital concentration led to divergent political reactions to external economic pressures.

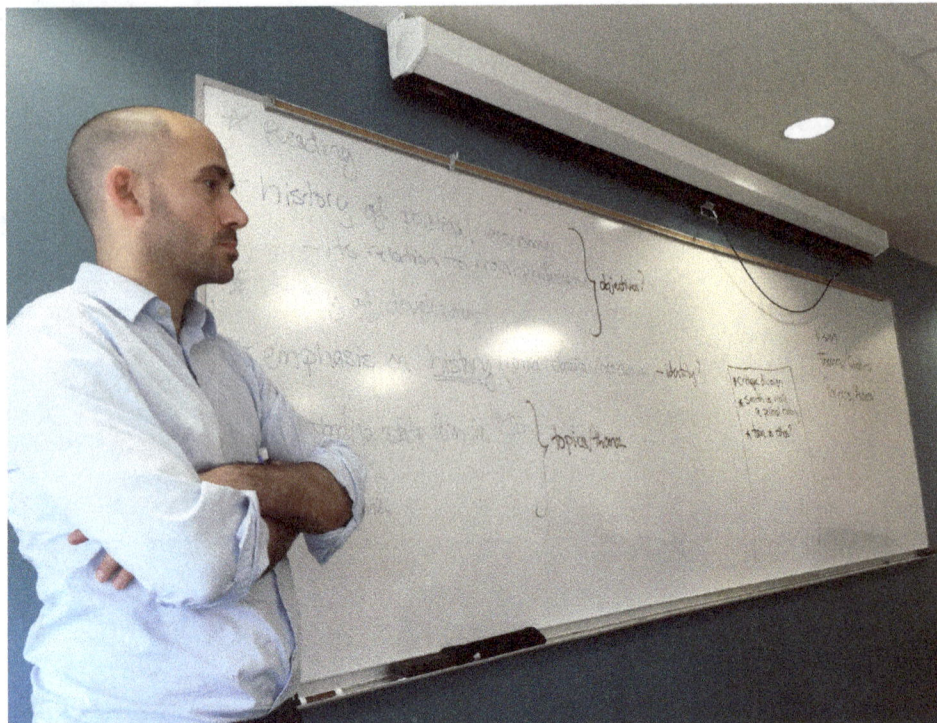

Ziad Abu-Rish at the Political Economy Project Founding Workshop. Image from the Arab Studies Institute.

Ishac Diwan and I recently published an updated version of Alan Richards and John Waterbury's *A Political Economy of the Middle East* (Westview Press, 2015). Our revisions have aimed to incorporate politics explicitly and integrally throughout the book. In most chapters we, therefore, emphasize the ways in which politics shape and are shaped by economic endowments and trends in the region. Our focus on "political settlements," which refer to the largely elite bargains that underlie political orders, is one way in which we do so. At present, we are working on an article that aims to explain distinct patterns of governance in the different types of political economies in the region using a deductive framework, descriptive statistics, and intra- and cross-regional comparative case studies.

I am a firm believer in methodological diversity and an opponent of methodological fundamentalism, and I adopt an eclectic approach to data collection and analysis. I consider myself a "mixed methods" researcher because, where possible and justified by the research question, the use of multiple methods increases confidence in our arguments and findings.

1. What do you consider good political economy texts and why?

Before beginning the doctoral program in political science at UC Berkeley, I had taken multiple development economics classes in which I was exposed to orthodox economic models and concepts based on variants of the "Washington consensus." At the time, I realized there was something missing in these accounts, but I was not quite sure how to think about markets differently. Like many people, I had a eureka moment when I first read Karl Polanyi's *The Great Transformation* (Beacon Press, 1944) at Berkeley. The contributions of this book are far too numerous to recount here, but I especially appreciate Polanyi's careful demonstration of the ways in which institutions (which are the product of specific political

struggles) shape economic behavior. A second piece, Kiren Chaudhry's "The Myths of the Market and the Common History of Late Developers" (*Politics & Society*, 1993), was also foundational for me. This article made clear the very political nature of market-making and emphasized the importance of capable state institutions for market exchange at a time when this was not yet the conventional wisdom. By now, mainstream economists have turned their lenses to institutions as the central driver of development processes, but Chaudhry and, of course, Polanyi, among others, made these points much earlier. More than many contemporary economists who study institutions, however, this vein of scholarship highlights the ways in which actual political struggles in real places shape and are shaped by institutions in an iterative fashion—an approach that makes sense to me.

In research on the political economy of development in the Middle East, I tend to gravitate toward works that adopt a political sociological approach and combine strong theory with careful attention to method and evidence. In my view, David Waldner's book, *State-Building and Late Development* (Cornell University Press, 1999), is a good example of this kind of approach. His account emphasizes the ways in which different patterns of coalition-building by political elites at independence shape political-economic institutions, which then produce distinct economic outcomes. Focusing on the Gulf states and on a distinct set of research questions, Steffan Hertog's piece in *World Politics* (2010), "Defying the Resource Curse," is a useful example of the ways in which case-based knowledge can be harnessed to make convincing critiques of the conventional wisdom (in this case, that state-owned enterprises are doomed to be inefficient and uncompetitive because of the alleged pathologies of public sector management).

Looking beyond work on the Middle East, I find Lily Tsai's work on public goods provision to be a model of good research marrying contextual knowledge with empirical rigor. In her book, *Accountability Without Democracy: Solidary Groups and Public Goods Provision in Rural China* (Cambridge University Press 2007), she shows how informal social ties affect the quality and extent of public goods provision. The book combines close knowledge of local social relations with a sophisticated and well-justified combination of research methods to make convincing and important arguments.

These are but a few examples of compelling scholarship, and I appreciate their marriage of theoretical and empirical rigor.

2. What are some of the pressing questions/concerns you would like to see (or avoid) in some or any agenda in political economy?

In political science much research on the Middle East has focused on the roots of persistent authoritarianism or Islamism. While these are productive and important research agendas, they may have crowded out work on other topics, which may be more germane to the interests of people in the region. I would like to see more research on economic and social outcomes in the region. Here are a few examples of potentially productive research questions:

a. Why and how have social welfare regimes evolved across diverse political economies in the region?

b. With the deconstruction of state forms and, in some cases, the rise of alternative poles of authority that directly challenge the state, what is at stake for people in the region? How do "ordinary people" meet their basic needs? What kinds of new political orders are emerging?

c. What do people expect of their states with respect to redistribution and social provision? Can we link public opinion with national or subnational patterns of development to discern distinct (or similar) sets of expectations vis-à-vis states in the region?

d. Beyond scholarly debates, our research can also adopt a more action-oriented approach to these issues. For example, can we devise prospective and creative approaches to improving living conditions and prospects for social mobility in Middle Eastern countries? What might a re-imagination of core political settlements look like–whether based on radical reformulations of social contracts and underlying foundations of political economies or marginal changes at the community-level? What can be done to address dire humanitarian crises in the region? What can and should scholars do?

3. What types of academic initiatives do you think could help in supporting and strengthening your work in PE, and help to push the field forward productively?

Here are a few ideas about initiatives that would help to strengthen our field and would enhance research programs on economic and social development in the Middle East:

a. The collection and organization of empirical data on economic and social policies: It is difficult to get comprehensive information on the types and range of social policies and reforms in countries across the region. A database searchable by country, sector, and time period would be especially valuable. A similar database that addresses economic policies across multiple sectors and organized in a similar format would also be a great resource for scholars, policy-makers, and activists alike. This would enable specialists on the region to engage more directly with the burgeoning scholarly literature on welfare regimes in developing countries, among other areas of inquiry. For policy-makers and activists, it would also facilitate more creative thinking about what approaches might be adopted to address pressing issues in the region and to improve living conditions.

b. Climate change and environmental threats in the Middle East: Climate change poses an especially grave threat to people in the Middle East, which has already begun to face its effects. More work should be done on this critical set of issues. To my knowledge, few scholars of the region work on environmental issues (although Jeannie Sowers and Toby Jones are two exceptions). Middle East specialists should participate more fully in this research agenda, which is increasingly important among social scientists specializing in other regions or in the political science subfield, international relations, and policy-makers in the region should devote more attention to this question.

c. I personally would value greater engagement between political scientists and economic historians of the Middle East, particularly given my new research agenda on the long-term historical roots of economic development in the region. I hope to foster more conversations across disciplinary and regional boundaries on the historical foundations of distinct development patterns in the Middle East.

Endnotes:
1. I use the term "Middle East" to refer to the MENA region as a whole.

POLITICAL ECONOMY PROJECT

Interrogating the dominant paradigms and providing insights for alternatives | Developing and encouraging critical approaches to political economy | Redefining "development," growth, redistribution, power relations, and social justice | To learn more or collaborate with the Political Economy Project (PEP), email info@politicaleconomyproject.com or visit www.politicaleconomyproject.org

Reclaiming Economics: Past and Possible Futures of Radical Political Economy

Omar Dahi

My understanding of political economy, which has both influenced my research and teaching, is shaped by two intellectual traditions both of which employ the political economy method to critique mainstream economic theory as well as capitalist development. The first is the tradition of radical political economy, institutionalist, feminist, and post-Keynesian economics that includes, among others, the works of Paul Sweezy, David Gordon, Richard Edward, Stephen Marglin, Michael Reich, Thomas Weisskopf, Julie Matthaei, William Dugger, Samuel Bowles, Julie Nelson, Julianne Malveaux, Joan Robinson, Hyman Minsky, and James Crotty.[1] The second is the tradition of neo-Marxian global political economy including world-systems analysis, structuralist and dependency theories, and North-South models of uneven development. Major works in this tradition include those by Raul Prebisch, Celso Furtado, William Darity, Jr., Samir Amin, Lance Taylor, Amitava Dutt, Jaime Ros, and others.[2]

The common denominator among all these approaches is that they see political economy as a method of analysis that incorporates history, power, and structures as key elements in understanding social reality. All of them generally see themselves as operating within an intellectual trajectory that traces back to Marx but are also generally critical of traditional or orthodox Marxism.

Sam Bowles presents a useful appreciation of these traditions of political economy; he defined radical political economy, particularly in the US tradition, as being at the intersection of three circles:[3] critiques of neoclassical economics (including critiques of methodological individualism, ahistorical and lack of institutional understanding, uni-causal explanations, perfect competition and market behavior, rational economic man, etc.); critiques of the topics that neoclassical economists focused on or avoided (including gender, race, imperialism, and financial instability); and a moral critique of capitalism (which includes both a critique of capitalism and working towards a transition towards a more just society).

What Bowles' exposition shows is that those of us whose academic training took place in economics departments have had to contend with the dominance of neoclassical economics. Maintaining a presence in the economics discipline for heterodox and radical political economists has been a largely losing battle in the United States as a result of a large scale assault on non-mainstream approaches within economics. I witnessed this battle first hand when I was a graduate student in economics at the University of Notre Dame in 20022003 when the administration voted to remove non-mainstream economists from the PhD-granting economics department, place them in an undergraduate only department, and several years later eliminate that department.[4] Such thought control and elimination of non-neoclassicals from economics departments, largely under the guise of increasing the academic ranking of the department, is what allowed Professor Jagdish Bhagwati

to glibly claim that "the anti-capitalist sentiments are particularly virulent among the young who arrive at their social awakening on campuses in fields other than economics. English, comparative literature, and sociology are fertile breeding grounds."[5]

This desire to remain in the discipline has created a bit of intellectual distance, I think, between political economists (or broadly heterodox economists) who are trained as economists, and our colleagues doing political economy work in other disciplines (history, sociology, anthropology, etc.). In order to avoid being pushed out of the discipline, i.e., to remain teaching in economics departments, a lot of our research engages with, or dwells on, refuting neoclassical theory, and much of our teaching usually mixes both mainstream and non-mainstream approaches in ways that are not always successful pedagogically from my experience. Our colleagues in other disciplines, free from such constraints (though obviously contending with many others), have been more interdisciplinary and, I think, more creative in the type of work they have produced.

> *Maintaining a presence in the economics discipline for heterodox and radical political economists has been a largely losing battle in the United States as a result of a large scale assault on non-mainstream approaches within economics.*

On the other hand, economists working in the political economy tradition continue to conduct valuable research that challenges the dominant orthodoxies on key issues relating to corporate power, trade agreements and investment treaties, financial markets, labor markets, and so on.

Four organizations or centers in the United States that I believe are exemplary of this type of work are the Political Economy Research Institute (PERI) at the University of Massachusetts in Amherst, the Center for Economic and Policy Research (CEPR) headed by Dean Baker and Mark Weisbrot, the Global Development and Environment Institute (GDAE) at Tufts University, and the Global Economic Governance Initiative (GEGI) at Boston University. Some of the research done by these organizations ranges from the impact of trade agreements and investment treaties, Chinese investments in Latin America, to gender and work, and the intersection between income inequality and toxic and low air quality living conditions. I have found the type of analysis produced by these centers incredibly valuable, particularly in my own research, which seeks to highlight the impact of different forms of economic exchange (e.g., trade, capital flows, tech exchange, and labor migration) between countries and regions on the distribution of power, and wealth as well, and broadly internal economic development within those regions.

In addition to bridging the gap between political economists from various disciplines, there are several practical ways in which the Political Economy Project can do very useful work along the lines of these programs. We can create pedagogically relevant material that highlights what we see as valuable political economy research taking place in the Middle East in order to better understand the emerging political and economic landscape in the Middle East and globally in the aftermath of the Great Recession as well as the Arab Uprisings. More broadly, we can contribute by assisting each other in developing teaching tools and ways to incorporate political economy research (not just about the Middle East) into our teaching. For example, the GDAE has developed a series of educational materials that includes textbooks, teaching modules, and other forms of instructor support. I have been involved with an initiative called Econ4 that seeks to achieve similar goals through the production of short instructional, and hopefully appealing, videos.

Second, we can develop ties with networks in the Middle East, which are usually working with on the ground development initiatives to conduct politically and socially relevant political economy research. One such network is the Arab NGO Network for Development (ANND). ANND, headed by Ziad Abdel Samad, commissions work on tax laws and tax reforms, labor rights including rights to unionize, as well as examination of trade policy, poverty, investment measures, and other issues. ANND serves as a watchdog in monitoring and providing a critical appraisal of development issues, is involved with developing partnerships and capacities with other organizations on this subject, and also helps set benchmarks for development that can be useful in policy battles in the region. In other regions of the developing world such analysis is usually developed in social science research centers such as CODESRIA in Africa, and CLACSO and FLACSO in Latin America. These institutes' counterpart in the Middle East, the newly formed Arab Council for Social Sciences in Beirut, does not yet have their research history but would be a perfect candidate with which to establish a partnership.

Finally, building on the work of Adam Hanieh and Shana Marshall, another useful initiative is building databases on North-South and South-South investment, joint ventures, and capital flows emanating or ending in the Middle East North Africa region.[6] This can be perhaps modeled along the lines of the China-Latin America investment database produced as a collaboration between GEGI and the Inter-American Dialogue initiative and which is both visually appealing and easy to use.

Endnotes:

1. P. Sweezy, *The Theory of Capitalist Development: Principles of Marxian Political Economy*, (New York: Monthly Review Press, 1970); R. Edwards, M. Reich, and T. Weisskopf, *The Capitalist System*, (New Jersey: Prentice Hall, 1978); W. Dugger, "Radical Institutionalism: Basic Concepts," *Review of Radical Political Economics* 20, no.2 (1988), 1-20; J. Crotty, "Are Keynesian Uncertainty and Macrotheory Compatible? Conventional Decision Making, Institutional Structures, and Conditional Stability in Keynesian Macromodels," in Gary Dymski and Robert Pollin, eds., *New Perspectives in Monetary Economics*, 105-139; J. Robinson, "Time in Economic Theory," *Kyklos* 33, (1980), 219-229; H. Minsky, "The Financial Instability Hypothesis: An Interpretation of Keynes and an Alternative to 'Standard' Theory," in Hyman P. Minsky, *Can 'It' Happen Again?* (1975), 59-70; J.

Malveaux. "Comparable Worth and Its Impact on Black Women," in Margaret C. Simms and Julianne Malveaux, eds. *Slipping Through the Cracks: The Status of Black Women*, 47-62; T. Amott and J. Matthaei, *Race, Gender, and Work: A Multicultural Economic History of Women in the United States*, (Boston: South End Press, 1991); S. Marglin, "What Do Bosses Do? The origins and functions of hierarchy in capitalist production," *Review of Radical Political Economics* 6(2) (1974), 60-112.

2. R. Prebisch, "Commercial Policy in Underdeveloped Countries," *The American Economic Review* 49, no. 2 (1959), 251-273; C. Furtado, *Economic Development Of Latin America: Historical Background and Contemporary Problems*, Cambridge University Press: Cambridge, 2nd edition (1990); I. Wallerstein. *The Modern World System*, Vols. I, II, and III; W. Jr. Darity, "A Model of 'Original Sin': Rise of the West and Lag of the Rest," *The American Economic Review* 82, no. 2(1992), 162-167; A. Dutt, The Origins of Uneven Development: the Indian Subcontinent," *The American Economic Review* 82, no. 2(1992), 146-150; L. Taylor, *Reconstructing Macroeconomics: Structuralist Proposals and Critiques of the Mainstream*, (Cambridge: Harvard University Press, 2004).

3. Sam Bowles and Stephen Resnick's lecture on radical economics and the UMass Amherst Department can be found here: https://www.youtube.com/watch?v=KDr1HCfxDKE. As Bowles argues, since the 1970s many economists who do not refer themselves as political economists or radical economists such as behavioralist economists and those working on microeconomics of development have since taken up many of those critiques employing experiments, agent-based modeling, randomized trials, and other approaches.

4. Some of the details of this outrageous process can be found at http://www.deirdremccloskey.com/editorials/notre.php, https://anticap.wordpress.com/2010/06/30/end-of-economics-and-policy-studies/, and https://anticap.wordpress.com/2010/03/08/it's-official-update-18/. The administration at the University of Notre Dame gave the department an ultimatum to make several changes, which included removing Political Economy and History of Economic Thought from the core curriculum of the Ph.D. program—or else the department would be frozen. When the department rejected the ultimatum, the department was indeed frozen before the split happened.

5. J. Bhagwati, *In Defense of Globalization*. (New York: Oxford University Press, 2004). David Colander and Arjo Klamer's classic *The Making Of An Economist* interviews graduate students in economics at elite universities to show the transformation of the discipline and its obsession with abstract modeling and econometric analysis.

6. Currently searching for investments requires multiple databases, for example through ESCWA ANIMA, and Dhaman.

JADMAG PEDAGOGY PUBLICATIONS ISSUE 4.2

Toward a Richly Textured Political Economy

Laleh Khalili

My graduate school response would have been "the set of social and economic relations that emerge from the interaction of the 'state,' 'capitalists,' and 'workers' and which affects the object called 'the economy'." "Capitalists" and "workers" could have been replaced by some other configuration of owners and workers of a particular mode of production.

But, of course, none of these terms are stable. Not just in our patch of scholarly research, but also in the vast majority of the world, the overlaps between the state and the owners of the mode of production are far too significant for these Weberian ideal-types to be useful in understanding how the economy works. Even "the economy" as an object of study is far too complex and constructed a subject to lend itself to this sort of heuristic simplification. Perhaps even more important is the challenge to the idea that "production" is only those sets of relationships that occur between owners of a mode of production and those whose labor is exploited by the owners. Feminists have exhorted us to understand (after Marx himself, really) the necessary forms of reproductive, caring, unpaid labor which are also absolutely necessary to the production of the system (here the work of Italian feminist autonomists like Fortunati and Federici is crucial).

So, for me, what I consider to be the object of "political economy" is far larger, far more amorphous, and far more dynamic and unpredictable than the things I learned in grad school a scant fifteen to twenty years ago. I think it would be far easier to delineate some of the parameters which, for me, define what political economy is:

1. It is today a study that not only looks at the "national" forms of socioeconomic relations, but also situates them transnationally, and that does not simply mean in relation to the former colonial metropoles or today's capitalist pivots, but also in relation to the global South, adjacent regions, and rising powers (Adam Hanieh's work, as well as Tim Mitchell's, Toby Jones's, and many others are indispensable in this regard).

2. It is also a recognition of the extraordinary work of social history in Middle East studies which incorporated the indispensable struggles over allocation and distribution of social goods and public benefits into the larger macro analyses of national and world economies (Zach Lockman, Joel Beinin, John Chalcraft, and a great many others are crucial here).

3. My own preference is increasingly for studies that show the inner workings of loci of politico-economic power. Maybe because these are areas of "expertise" where specialized knowledge is used to shield the apparatuses of power from scrutiny. Much more work is needed here, but I think older works such as Tetreault's book on the Kuwait Petroleum Company, and new research on the making of infrastructures (Elyachar on infrastructure in Egypt and Stamatopolous-Robbins on waste

in Palestine), specific product markets (for example Caliskan's work on cotton production and supply chain), specific sectors (tourism for example; Hazbun's work here is instructive), and finance are necessary (here, although Timur Kuran's work is hugely problematic, it is also in some senses pioneering).

There is so much more work to be done within the field in any case. While Ottoman historians seem to be miles ahead on their delineation of the historical emergence of local, regional, and global economies that passed through the Ottoman Empire, much else remains puzzling, unexplored, and excitingly open to study. Nearly ten years ago, when I put together a compendium of works on Middle East studies, I was struck by how much Egypt was a locus of exploration and research among Arab states, and how much research about other countries of the Middle East (and that included Israel, Turkey, and Iran) were focused on geopolitics and politics of security (but in a very mundane and mainstream sort of way).

> *While Ottoman historians seem to be miles ahead on their delineation of the historical emergence of local, regional, and global economies that passed through the Ottoman Empire, much else remains puzzling, unexplored, and excitingly open to study.*

My own sense is that the innovative and new ways in which people are incorporating science studies; the recent "return" to studies of capitalism (however Euro/US-centric these may be at the moment); and the recent anthropological turn to infrastructures all can be exciting developments for the study of political economy. For me, and my recent obsession with ports etc., I also think urban studies, the study of supply-chains, and understanding the traffic between commerce and war are incredibly useful ways to frame and understand the development of that largely invisible sector, transport. For me, dissecting the mechanisms of power, exchange, extraction, and reproduction embedded in logistics and transport industries provides an arena via which I will get to study finance; construction; environmental degradation; labor exploitation; and a global movement of goods, peoples, and capital. I tend not to be particularly committed to any one frame, though of course I am deeply influenced by Marxian understandings of production and valorization. I feel like I am a magpie, eclectic in my interests and excited by my gradual understanding of different aspects of the making of global capitalism. I think there is room for both macro and micro analytics of this system, and for different approaches, because its flexibility, suppleness, and resilience need to be understood at multiple levels, and from a range of angles, in order to be better challenged.

What is Political Economy?

Toufic Haddad

Political economy has the potential to offer students and educators valuable explanatory insights on the Middle East and the world at large. Realizing this potential, however, requires gaining a better command of what political economy is, how it is distinct from other disciplines that deal with similar subjects, as well as what the various streams and practices within the tradition of political economy are.

Broadly speaking, political economy is concerned with understanding the sets of relationships between politics and economics within a particular geographical, temporal, and social setting. At its core is a concern for the mutually constitutive processes and interactions between "political" interests, the organization and balance of power and social relationships on the one hand, and "economic" structure and activity on the other.

Different intellectual traditions approach the study of these relations from different assumptive bases, and hence derive different conclusions to economic, political, and social concerns. These explanations in turn inform a range of activities societies and governments undertake, including the crafting of future policy interventions and the assigning of forms of moral culpability.

Two main approaches fundamentally divide the political economy tradition.

Liberal traditions uphold the assumption that individuals are rationally calculating individuals who seek utility self-maximization. Their decisions are individually determined on the basis of an existing incentive structures and market signals. In attempting to craft explanations and solutions to political and economic problems, the liberal tradition focuses on deficiencies of the structure of incentives that the individual exists within and which s/he responds to, as a means to unleash in an axiomatic and rational deductive manner, processes that lead to utility maximization. Centrality is given to independent human agency in determining political/or economic will or interest, which is exercised efficiently in the pursuit of individual wellbeing.

Heterodox traditions uphold that the conditions of social reproduction; the modes of production at the heart of this reproduction; and the social classes generated as part of this process, collectively inform and determine the kinds of consciousness that arise and find receptivity, traction, and salience within a given sociopolitical and temporal order. Individual deci-

sion making is hence seen as shaped and constrained by inherited structures, social forces, and habits forged in collective experiences. Rather than individual agency taking place in a manner that is purely individual and calculative, the heterodox tradition stresses a relational rationality or habitual decision making.

Thus, in attempting to craft explanations and solutions to political and economic problems, the heterodox tradition tends to shed light on the character of the conditions of social reproduction itself–its inequalities, disparities, inefficiencies, and patterning as experienced through social classes, and as a consequence of politically influenced bonds and ties. The organization and structure of the modes of production that facilitate social reproduction, and the relations this generates between groups is central to the heterodox tradition. Thus, understanding the "who" and "how" of accumulation is pivotal.

The assumptive basis in which scholars approach political economy goes a distance to determining one's methodological approach to the discipline itself, and the answers and policies generated from this analysis.

My personal affinity in political economy lies with the heterodox tradition. That is to say, I conceive of political economy as an attempt to construct a reading of material factors—both natural and man-made—that shape the social, political, and economic order, and the modes of production that have arisen therein that sustain and reproduce societies. Given that we live in an era of capitalist production, it becomes a study of the particular character of a capitalist order in a given context: analyzing objective structural factors of the economic, infrastructural, and geographic/topographic order; the modes of production that have historically arisen there; the various constellations of forces and social classes that engage in this reproduction and how; and the political character and com-

Participants and members at the PEP Founding Workshop. Image from the Arab Studies Institute.

position of these formations, their power, and patterning relative to one another etc.

Equally important to conducting this analysis is situating the local context within broader regional and international dynamics related to capitalist circulation and reproduction. This necessarily entails incorporating an analysis of relevant imperial and geostrategic factors given that capitalism has already generated established hierarchies among states and the ways they project, sustain, reproduce, and expand their power.

> I conceive of political economy as an attempt to construct a reading of material factors— both natural and man-made—that shape the social, political, and economic order, and the modes of production that have arisen therein that sustain and reproduce societies.

Legal factors must equally be considered given how the law is a key historical institution that has served to regulate social and economic relations and corresponding balances of power between social groups and classes. The history of its generation says a lot about this power balance.

Reflecting upon the material, economic, and institutional order (both local and international) which helped create, shape, and sustain a given reality must necessarily give special attention to the particular power balance and tensions this relies upon and generates between social, political, and economic actors/ groups, domestic and international. Who benefits, in what way, and at the expense of whom, and how? On top of this arises the question of how governance itself is imposed and legitimated, which begins to bring in questions of ideology and political or cultural hegemony, and the means by which this is generated as well.

The task of the political economist is thus to ride the dynamic tension between structural and material factors on the one hand, and the factors of political consciousness and agency on the other, formulating a reading of how the former shapes the latter, only to have the latter reshape the former. Attention to this dynamic and dialectical process of shaping and reshaping the world is central to the heterodox political economy tradition, always embarking on one's methodological approach from the incontrovertible material realities which shape social reproduction and hence social relations, and not from the ideas themselves. This process of explaining is delicate and must always shy away from mechanistic approaches that are deterministic and deny agency to actors and groups. The political will always have autonomy as a function of free will. At the same time, the salient ideas of a given social context cannot be divorced from the pressing conditions that determine social reproduction, including the need for societies to fulfill basic needs of security and wellbeing within a given socio-temporal existence.

This is the delicate challenge of political economy: to capture descriptively–quantitatively and qualitatively–how incontro-

vertible objective material conditions and factors, construct the social and inform its political bases, doing so without denying agency or ignoring material or immaterial factors that structure and inform reproduction. There is no formulaic manner in which this task can be undertaken given the specific historicized nature of a given context, let alone the impossibility of attempting to "freeze" for a moment in time, all the dynamic and evolving factors taking place in a given context. Still political economists must attempt to use the tools at their disposal to construct an account of the factors that help to explain whatever is being investigated or explained, without over-extending one's analysis to the point of hubristic determinism and omniscience.

While quantitative and qualitative means are equally beneficial to this descriptive process, less important to the specific method used is the incontrovertible nature of the observations and relations captured. With this noted, there may be a particular value found in attempting to capture given phenomenon through forms of quantification given their ability to frontally challenge the whitewashing character of so much mainstream economics. There are plenty of valid critiques of mainstream economics and its preassumptions, rooted in the neoclassical worldview—with its utopian conceptions of the universe that selectively frame, elide, and justify capitalist accumulation and reproduction. Yet the economic indicators of this discipline can still be used to construct powerful counter critiques to capitalist hegemony and configurations. Heterodox political economy should not shy away from engaging with these tools, and should even be encouraged to apply them, as powerful counter-critiques that paint a portrait of how this system of accumulation exploits and oppresses, not only qualitatively but also quantitatively. At the same time, qualitative tools and methods of describing and illustrating these relations mechanisms and dynamics can equally compliment the portrait being constructed. All this is to emphasize that there is no reason why the powerful illustrative tools employed by mainstream economics–even with their known caveats–should be left in the hands of mainstream economists. Mainstream economics can be challenged with the same means used to uphold it, in addition to critiques, which emerge from disclosing the false assumptions and elisions typical to its practice.

Collectively these ideas frame the biases in my preference for political economic texts and my own approach in political economic analysis. I subsequently search out texts, data, and phenomenon that trace, characterize, and illustrate the architecture of capitalist production within a given context, situating this context as a function of global, regional, and local specificities; the economic, legal, and political regimes that have arisen around the social classes; and the political formations engaged in these processes.

Applying heterodox political economic analyses to the Middle East context can be particularly helpful in explaining the processes underway there, as they go a considerable distance in explaining the context from which social and political ideas and movements arise. This has only been underscored with the upheavals of the region since 2011, where the overall developmental context of the Arab world, and the political economic orders established therein– characterized overwhelmingly by neopatrimonial and patrimonial rentier states–help to explain the eruption of revolutions, the resilience of the ancien regimes, and the complexity of the processes underway. This includes insights into the historical patterning of the social benefactors of these regimes and how this overlaps with various identities of different orders. Without a political economic analysis of these problems, the tendency to look at complicated phenomenon like sectarianism through ideological and ideational lenses can easily lead to reproducing various orientalist and dehumanizing mantras that neither adequately explain these phenomenon nor meet the moral obligation generated by scholarship that injustice should be exposed and redressed.

> *Without a political economic analysis of these problems, the tendency to look at complicated phenomenon like sectarianism through ideological and ideational lenses can easily lead to reproducing various Orientalist and dehumanizing mantras that neither adequately explain these phenomenon nor meet the moral obligation generated by scholarship that injustice should be exposed and redressed.*

It is also worth noting that it is not by accident that the powerful western states engaged in practices of peacebuilding, statebuilding, and international development, together with international financial institutions like the World Bank and International Monetary Fund—that all of these explicitly or implicitly rely upon forms of political economic analysis when it comes to analyzing a given political context and formulating their policy interventions therein. While the most intimate details of these analyses are certainly kept to their inner policy formulators, extensive paper trails of their ap-

proach and methodologies have become explicit. For example, the 2011 World Development Report "Conflict Security and Development" produced by the World Bank goes into detail regarding how development and stability can be engineered, while describing the evolving consensuses on "elite pacts," "political settlements," and "inclusive enough coalitions." That is to say, contemporary developmental practice has become increasingly up front about attempting to socially and politically engineer certain outcomes, using the neoliberal doctrines as a convenient framework to guise these practices. It should be well understood that the manipulation of the political economy of a given region is the very modus operandi of these organizations and institutions, with the goal of the scholar to unpackage how that takes place, and how the official transcript imparts or disguises these processes.

In any case, while there will always be inherent limitations to all disciplines, respect for a political economic tradition rooted in understanding the structural objective factors that frame the organization of a material reality and constrain agency will always be worth maintaining. This is because, whether we recognize it or not, social and political orders must always be materially undergirded to be sustained. The character and nature of this reproduction, and the forces required to maintain it, fundamentally go to the heart of political economy itself, be this for state and non-state actors alike. The role of the scholar is to discern how this takes place on both macro and micro levels, and should be practiced with the view that an equitable, and less oppressive order should be sought.

Interviewing
activists, journalists, citizens + scholars
to address salient issues
in the Middle East

الوضع
Status
AUDIO JOURNAL
مجلة صوتية

statushour.com

JADMAG PEDAGOGY PUBLICATIONS ISSUE 4.2

A Critical Political Economy: Social Forms, Power Relations, and Alternatives

Mandy Turner

A critical political economy should focus on decoding social forms, demystifying power relations, and highlighting alternatives—for both the general and the particular. The key task of the critical researcher is to puncture "common sense" understandings that protect and reproduce hegemonic ideas and structures. My overall framework is, thus, one informed by a broadly Marxist and Gramscian perspective based on a conceptualization of "the social world as a constant making and unmaking of social structures of human needs and capacities—structures that are constructed through the conflictual encounter between what we call social movements from above and social movements from below."[1] The use of the terms "social movements from above" and "social movements from below" allows us to widen our conceptualization of struggle beyond that between capital and labor, and it is this constant "conflictual encounter," over the maintenance or opposition to a dominant structure of needs and capacities, which creates a social formation at any given point.[2] Social structures and political formations are the outcome and sediment of (ongoing) struggles. This is how I would understand the political economy of the postwar Keynesian consensus and the post-1980s neoliberal offensive, for instance. A critical political economy of the Middle East, therefore, should understand social change and historical transformation as a living process; we must continually acknowledge the possibility that structures will be constituted in a different way. Our theories and concepts should, therefore, be historical and dynamic, and guided by praxis.

> *A critical political economy of the Middle East, therefore, should understand social change and historical transformation as a living process; we must continually acknowledge the possibility that structures will be constituted in a different way.*

This perspective has meant that I am more tended towards texts that analyze the constant making and unmaking of social structures through conflictual encounters. Some examples of this approach in books specifically on the Middle East include: Hannah Batatu, *The Old Social Classes and the Revolutionary Movement in Iraq*, Saqi, 2004; Joel Beinin and Zachary Lockman, *Workers on the Nile: Nationalism, Communism, Islam and the Egyptian Working Class*, 1882-1954, American University in Cairo Press, 1988; Ellis Goldberg, *Tinker, Tailor and Textile Worker: Class and Politics in Egypt*, 1930-1952, Berkeley, University of California Press, 1986; Gershon Shafir, *Land, Labor and the Origins of the Israeli-Palestinian Conflict*, 1882-1914, University of California Press, 1988; Ray Bush, *Counter-revolution in Egypt's Countryside: Land and Farmers in the Era of Reform*, Zed Books, 2002. For me, these capture the essence of the type of political economy research to which I aspire.

Research on Palestine I: The General and the Particular

This overall framework guides my research on Palestine in the following ways. First, through an analysis of the general context—i.e., the Palestinian people as a stateless population geographically fragmented but experiencing a common and ongoing process of dispossession, disenfranchisement, and disarticulation. A critical political economy of the Palestinian people needs to critique and transcend the colonizer's discourse that has divided and fragmented them into separate and distinct groups (some thereafter named as "Arab-Israeli," "Bedouin," and so on; recently we have even heard the term "Gazans"). This understanding of the general context should always be borne in mind when analyzing particular contexts—i.e., how the general political economy of the Palestinian people has fragmented into specific localities, the way in which these have developed, the power relations within each context, and the potential for transformation. My recent co-edited book, *Decolonizing Palestinian Political Economy: De-development and Beyond* (PalgraveMacmillan, 2014; with Omar Shweiki) brought together experts across the field of Palestine studies in order to analyze the shared experience of marginalization and dispossession in different contexts. This book sought to critique and transcend the invisible colonial grammar that takes these different contexts for granted and reifies them, while also recognizing the challenges thrown up by different contexts. The starting point was the application, to particular contexts, of Sara Roy's concept of "de-development," defined as "the deliberate, systematic and progressive dismemberment of an indigenous economy by a dominant one, where economic—and by extension, societal—potential is not only distorted but denied."[3] All contributions presented a bleak picture, but they also suggested ways forward out of the malaise of each "conflictual encounter."

Research on Palestine II: Decoding Western Peacebuilding in the Occupied Palestinian Territories

My individual research and publications have largely specifically focused on western donor practices in the Occupied Palestinian Territories (OPT) since the signing of the Oslo Peace Accord between Israel and the Palestine Liberation Organization (PLO) in 1993. This is a product of my general research interest and background in the cause and consequences of western intervention and the political economy of donor peacebuilding.[4] My research decodes western donor language and policies generally as a product of development fashions formed by liberal prejudices on the nature of conflict and peace, and specifically in the OPT as a product of their analysis of the "conflict."[5] The majority of research and writing on donors in the OPT has focused on critiquing them for failing to develop the OPT or to deliver peace—and it is important to do this (as does some of my earlier work).[6] However, I have recently offered a different type of critique—one that proposes a general understanding of western peacebuilding as a form of counterinsurgency practice and a specific understanding of how its application in the OPT operates as another layer of pacification techniques that compliment and mesh with the structures of domination and repression created by Israel, and which have helped to create a particular form of political economy that stabilizes *from the inside* in partnership with Palestinian elites who benefit from its implementation. Up until now, I have focused on western strategies and their impacts in the realms of development assistance, governance strategies, and security coordination in the OPT, but there is a need to examine these in conjunction with an in-depth analysis of the political economy of the OPT which has changed dramatically over the past twenty years and has instituted societal changes that have intensified since 2007.

Research on Palestine III: The Political Economy of Quasi-statehood Under Occupation

In partnership with Tariq Dana (Birzeit University), I am about to embark on a two-year research project entitled "The political economy of quasi-statehood under occupation: political allegiances and economic alliances in the occupied Palestinian territory of the West Bank" (funded by the LSE Middle East Centre). The research will build on the work of Mushtaq H. Khan and Markus E. Bouillon in its focus on articulating the interconnections between political and economic power in the OPT, and specifically the changes that have taken place in the past eight years.[7] It also seeks to build and expand on the important work of Adam Hanieh in identifying Palestinian capitalists as a subsection of Gulf capital,[8] but to explore this in greater depth. The research will highlight the distinctive nature of Palestinian business elite formation, which neither emerged in terms of relations of production within the OPT, nor developed within specific national boundaries governed by a sovereign nation-state. In fact, understanding the increasing centrality of the Palestinian business elite today–particularly returnees–requires further investigation into its diasporic origin and the complex network of capital accumulation on regional and international levels.

A central aim of this project is to examine the ways in which certain economic actors and business interest groups have been influencing the policies and decision-making process of the Palestinian Authority since its establishment in 1994, and how (if at all) this influence has increased since 2007. Our research questions include the following: What are the factors that facilitated the political influence of economic groups? Which mechanisms are being used by economic groups to influence PA policies? What are the wider political consequences of the interconnections between these economic actors and the political establishment? How does this contribute to shaping the new political economy of the occupied West Bank? How has this specifically related to Palestinian neoliberal approaches to state-building and economic development at this historical moment? Another important objective of the research project is to explore if and how Palestinian capital is linked and integrated into Israeli capital.

Our aim is to develop greater clarity on the relationship between political and economic power and the particular form of development taking place in the OPT, Israeli-Palestinian relations, as well as internal Palestinian dynamics and its dependency on regional and international configurations. We hope that our findings will help develop the basis for a new political economy perspective on dynamics embedded within the "Oslo peace paradigm," which may advance ongoing debates on the relationship between the

structure of power and economic interests in the context of quasi-statehood under occupation.

Key Concerns for a Critical Political Economy of the Middle East (and the OPT)

The key questions and concerns for a critical political economy of the Middle East are no different than those for other parts of the world, in my opinion, i.e., How do we understand the political economy of capitalism in its current neoliberal form? How has it manifested specifically in the Middle East? And what are the potentials for resistance and change?

Over the past twenty years, the Arab world has been experiencing two major ongoing transformative processes: first, the adoption of neoliberal policies and the resultant societal changes; and second, the revolutions and counter-revolutions that have been sweeping across the region since 2010. The historic defeat of Arab socialism and the processes of accumulation by dispossession that came in its wake have created particular dynamics that continue to unfold. "Conflictual encounters" between social movements from above and social movements from below continue, and how this will develop remains an open question. Collaborative work that brings together specialists from different fields of Middle East studies (not just political economists) is likely to bear the most fruit for the development of new concepts, theories and analyses of these two transformative processes. This is because political economy should not be regarded as a separate sphere of research, but understood as deeply embedded in the debates of other disciplines such as sociology, anthropology, history, and geography.

Specifically, for the OPT, (which has had no revolutionary moment, but has experienced lots of fragmented social movements from below), research should focus on the following areas.

1. The political economy of Israel (and its occupation).

There have been some useful analyses, specifically by Shir Hever and Jonathan Nitzan and Shimshon Bichler, but more needs to be done.[9] It is crucial to understand Israel's political economy and how this might (or might not) affect its relationship with the Palestinian people, its form of settler colonialism, its relationship (and support) from other countries,[10] as well as the possibility for change. What is the potential for the emergence of a social movement from below to challenge Zionism, and from where?

2. The political economy of a people experiencing settler colonialism.

We need to decipher the power and class relations in the Palestinian communities fragmented into local contexts due to the impacts of Israel's settler colonialism. This will be different and specific for the West Bank, the Gaza Strip, East Jerusalem, and the Palestinians inside Israel (as well as different refugee communities).

3. The political economy of resistance.

We need to critically analyze the policies and practices of Palestinian political leaders and parties in all of the local contexts. Are there any alternatives? Can the current fragmented social move-

JADMAG PEDAGOGY PUBLICATIONS ISSUE 4.2

ments from below across the Palestinian body politic come together to institute change?

> *Collaborative work that brings together specialists from different fields of Middle East studies (not just political economists) is likely to bear the most fruit for the development of new concepts, theories and analyses.*

In my opinion, any type of partnerships, joint work, or workshops that bring critical political economists from across the region together for discussion, debate, and comparative analysis will be useful for the cross-fertilization of ideas, concepts, and empirical knowledge. However, one very useful initiative that this group could consider would be to find sponsorship for a textbook of key readings in political economy to be translated into Arabic, as there is a dearth of books on political economy which makes teaching the subject to students very difficult.

Endnotes:

1. Alf Gunvald Nilsen and Laurence Cox, "What Would A Marxist Theory of Social Movements Look Like?" in *Marxism and Social Movements*, edited by Colin Barker, John Krinsky and Alf Gunvald Nilsen (Leiden: Brill, 2013), 63-81; 65.

2. Nilsen and Cox, (2013), 65.

3. Sara Roy, *Failing Peace: Gaza and the Palestinian-Israeli Conflict*, (London: Pluto Press, 2007).

4. Mandy Turner and Florian Kühn (eds.), *The Politics of International Intervention: The Tyranny of Peace*, (Routledge, forthcoming, 2015); Michael Pugh, Neil Cooper and Mandy Turner (eds.), *Whose Peace?: Critical Perspectives on the Political Economy of Peacebuilding*, (Basingstoke: PalgraveMacmillan, 2008/2011); Neil Cooper, Michael Pugh and Mandy Turner, "The End of History and the Last Liberal Peacebuilder: A Reply to Roland Paris," *Review of International Studies* 37(3), (2011), 1995-2007.

5. Mandy Turner, "The Power of "Shock and Awe": The Palestinian Authority and the Road to Reform," *International Peacekeeping* 16, no.4 (2009), 562–77; Mandy Turner, "Creating "Partners for Peace": the Palestinian Authority and the International Statebuilding Agenda," *Journal of Intervention and Statebuilding* 4, no.1 (2011), 1-21; Mandy Turner, "Security, Cooptation and Resistance: Peaebuilding-as-Fragmentation in the occupied Palestinian territory," in Oliver P. Richmond and Audra Mitchell (eds.) *Hybrid Forms of Peace: From the 'Everyday' to Post-Liberalism*, (Basingstoke: PalgraveMacmillan, 2011): 188-207; Mandy Turner, "Statebuilding in Palestine: Caught Between Occupation, Realpolitik and the Liberal Peace," in David Chandler and Timothy D. Sisk (eds.), *Routledge Handbook of International Statebuilding* (Abingdon: Routledge, 2013); Mandy Turner, "The political economy of western aid in the occupied Palestinian territory since the Oslo Accord," *Decolonizing Palestinian Political Economy*, 2014, op cit; Mandy Turner, "Completing the circle: peacebuilding as colonial practice in the occupied Palestinian territory," International Peacekeping 19(5), (2012), 492-507; Mandy Turner, "Peacebuilding in Palestine: Western Strategies in a Context of Colonisation," in Karim Makdisi and Vijay Prashad (eds.), *Land of Blue Helmets: the UN in the Arab World*, (University of California Press, 2015); Mandy Turner, "Securing and Stabilising: Peacebuilding as Counterinsurgency in the Occupied Palestinian Territory," *The Politics of International Intervention*, (2015), op cit, forthcoming.

6. Anne Le More, *International Assistance to the Palestinians After Oslo: Political Guilt*, Wasted Money, (Oxon: Routledge, 2008); Mushtaq H. Khan, George Giacaman and Inge Amundsen (eds.) *State Formation in Palestine: Viability and Governance During a Social Transformation*, (Abingdon: Routledge Curzon, 2004); Sara Roy, *Failing Peace: Gaza and the Palestinian-Israeli conflict*, (London: Pluto Press, 2007); Sahar Taghdisi-Rad, *The Political Economy of Aid in Palestine: Relief from Development or Development Delayed?*, (London: Routledge, 2011.)

7. Mushtaq H. Khan, George Giacaman and Inge Amundsen (eds.) *State Formation in Palestine: Viability and Governance During a Social Transformation*, (Abingdon: Routledge Curzon, 2004); Markus E. Bouillon *The Peace Business: Money and Power in the Palestine-Israel Conflict*, (London: IB Tauris, 2006).

8. Adam Hanieh, "The Internationalisation of Gulf Capital and Palestinian Class Formation." *Capital and Class* 35 (1) (2011), 81-106; Adam Hanieh, *Lineages of Revolt: Issues of Contemporary Capitalism in the Middle East*, (Chicago: Haymarket, 2013).

9. Shir Hever, *The Political Economy of Israel's Occupation*, (Pluto Press, 2010); Jonathan Nitzan and Shimshon Bichler, *The Global Political Economy of Israel*, (Pluto Press, 2002).

10. Jeff Halper's forthcoming book, *War Against the People: Israel, the Palestinians and Global Pacification*, (Pluto Press, 2015), analyzes Israel as a niche in the "global pacification economy" through its production, testing, and training of counterinsurgency/counter-terrorism measures, tools, and forces.

About the Authors

Joel Beinin is the Donald J. McLachlan professor of history and professor of Middle East history at Stanford University. His research and writing focus on modern and contemporary Egypt, Israel, Palestine, the Arab-Israeli conflict, political Islam, and US policy in the Middle East. Beinin has written or edited nine books, most recently *Social Movements, Mobilization, and Contestation in the Middle East and North Africa* (Stanford University Press, 2011), co-edited with Frédéric Vairel; *The Struggle for Worker Rights in Egypt* (Solidarity Center, 2010); and *Workers and Peasants in the Modern Middle East* (Cambridge University Press, 2001). His articles have been published in leading scholarly journals as well as *The Nation*, *Le Monde Diplomatique*, *Middle East Report*, *The Los Angeles Times*, *The San Francisco Chronicle*, *The San Jose Mercury News*, *The San Diego Union-Tribune*, *The Jordan Times*, *Asia Times*, and several blogs.

Melani Cammett is a professor of government at Harvard University. Cammett's recent books include *Compassionate Communalism: Welfare and Sectarianism in Lebanon* (Cornell University Press, 2014), which explores how politics shape the distribution of welfare goods by ethnic and sectarian organizations, and *A Political Economy of the Middle East* (co-authored with Ishac Diwan, Westview Press 2015), which analyzes the interplay of economic, political, and social factors in economic and social development in the region. Her co-edited book, *The Politics of Non-State Social Welfare in the Global South* (Cornell University Press, 2014), examines the origins, evolution and consequences of non-state welfare provision for state-building and human security in diverse regions. Cammett's current research projects explore governance and the politics of social service provision by public, private and non-state actors in the Middle East and identity politics in the region. She is also beginning a new project on the long-term historical roots of distinct development trajectories in the Middle East. Cammett has also published numerous articles in academic and policy journals and consults for development policy organizations.

Omar Dahi is an associate professor of economics at Hampshire College. He specializes in economic development and international trade, with a focus on South-South economic relations and the political economy of the Middle East and North Africa. Dahi's work has been published in various academic journals, including the *Journal of Development Economics*, *Applied Economics*, and the *Southern Economic Journal*. Dahi also serves on the editorial team of the *Middle East Report* and is co-editor of the Syria page at *Jadaliyya*.

Bassam Haddad is director of the Middle East Studies Program and associate professor at the School of Policy, Government, and International Affairs (SPGIA) at George Mason University. He is the author of *Business Networks in Syria: The Political Economy of Authoritarian Resilience* (Stanford University Press, 2011) and co-editor of *Dawn of the Arab Uprisings: End of an Old Order?* (Pluto Press, 2012). Bassam is currently writing his second book on *Understanding the Syrian Tragedy: The Long View* (Stanford Press) and teaches a staple graduate seminar at Georgetown University on "The Politics of Syria." He serves as founding editor of the *Arab Studies Journal*, a peer-reviewed research publication, and is co-producer/director of the award-winning documentary film, *About Baghdad*, and director of a critically acclaimed film series on *Arabs and Terrorism*, based on extensive field research and interviews. Bassam is co-founder/editor of *Jadaliyya* Ezine and the executive director of the *Arab Studies Institute*, an umbrella for five organizations dealing with knowledge production on the Middle East. He serves on the Board of the Arab Council for the Social Sciences and is executive producer of *Status* Audio Journal.

Toufic Haddad recently completed his PhD in Development Studies at the School for Oriental and African Studies (SOAS) in London. His doctoral research focused on the political economy of neoliberal approaches to conflict resolution and statebuilding in the Occupied Palestinian Territory from 1993-2013. It has recently been transformed into a manuscript and is under review for publication. Previous to enrolling in his PhD, Haddad worked in various capacities across the Occupied Palestinian Territory, including as a journalist, researcher, editor, and publisher. He also worked in various NGOs (Badil Center for Residency and Refugee Rights; the Alternative Information Center) and INGOs (UNOCHA and UNDP).

Adam Hanieh is a lecturer in the Development Studies Department of the School of Oriental and African Studies (SOAS), University of London. He is author of the forthcoming book, *Capitalism and Class in the Gulf Arab States* (Palgrave Macmillan, 2011). His book, *Lineages of Revolt: Issues of Contemporary Capitalism in the Middle East*, was published by Haymarket Press in September 2013.

Laleh Khalili is a professor of Middle East politics at SOAS, University of London, and the author of *Heroes and Martyrs of Palestine: The Politics of National Commemoration* (Cambridge, 2007) and *Time in the Shadows: Confinement in Counterinsurgencies* (Stanford 2013). She has also edited *Modern Arab Politics* (Routledge, 2008) and co-edited (with Jillian Schwedler) *Policing and Prisons in the Middle East: Formations of Coercion* (Hurst/OUP 2010). *Time in the Shadows* was the winner of the Susan Strange Best Book Prize of the British International Studies Association and the 2014 best book award of the International Political Sociology section of the ISA. Khalili's most recent research project engages the politics and political economy of war and militaries as it intersects with infrastructure, logistics and transport with specific focus on the Middle East.

Shana Marshall is associate director of the Institute for Middle East Studies and research faculty member at the George Washington University's Elliott School of International Affairs. She earned her PhD in International Relations and Comparative Politics of the Middle East at the University of Maryland in 2012. Her dissertation "The New Politics of Patronage: The Arms Trade and Clientelism in the Arab World" (forthcoming, Columbia University Press) examines how Middle East governments use arms sales agreements to channel financial resources and economic privileges to pro-regime elites. Her work has appeared in *The Middle East Report* (MERIP), *The International Journal of Middle East Studies*, *Middle East Policy*, *Jadaliyya*, and the *Carnegie Middle East Center*.

Sherene Seikaly is associate professor of History at the University of California, Santa Barbara. Previously she was assistant professor of History and director of the Middle East Studies Center at the American University in Cairo. She is the editor of the *Arab Studies Journal* and co-founder and editor of *Jadaliyya* e-zine. Seikaly's *Men of Capital: Scarcity and Economy in Mandate Palestine* (Stanford University Press, 2015) explores how Palestinian capitalists and British colonial officials used economy to shape territory, nationalism, the home, and the body.

Mandy Turner is the director of the Kenyon Institute (Council for British Research in the Levant) in East Jerusalem and a visiting research fellow at the Middle East Centre, London School of Economics (LSE). Previous positions include lecturer in Conflict Resolution at the University of Bradford (UK) and teaching fellow at University College London. Before entering academia, she was a journalist with *The Guardian* newspaper in London. Turner's research and publications focus thematically on the politics of intervention, and the political economy of peace building and development in conflict and war-torn societies, with a country focus on the occupied Palestinian territory.

The **Editors**

Ziad Abu-Rish is assistant professor in the Department of History at Ohio University. He specializes in the modern Middle East, and his research interests focus on the political economy and cultural constructions of state formation in the Levant. Abu-Rish is the author of "Garbage Politics in Lebanon" (*Middle East Report*) and "Protest, Regime Stability, and State Formation in Jordan" (*Beyond the Arab Spring: The Evolving Ruling Bargain*). He is also co-editor of *The Dawn of the Arab Uprisings: End of An Old Order?* (Pluto Press, 2012). Abu-Rish serves on the editorial teams of both the Arab Studies Journal and Jadaliyya e-zine.

Joel Beinin (biography above)

Omar Dahi (biography above)

Bassam Haddad (biography above)

Sherene Seikaly (biography above)

Annotated Bibliography

One of the main initiatives of the Political Economy Project (PEP) is the annotated bibliography project, which is designed to complement PEP's other pedagogy resources, and which will be disseminated through the network and published online for others to use. The project seeks to compile and annotate key political economy texts and classify them in ways that are easily accessible and useful to both scholars and educators. The texts range from classic and seminal texts to historical case studies, to contemporary political economy analysis within the Middle East. The selections we have included here are a sub-set of the total number of annotations completed so far. In the first section, we selected a few citations from the essays included in the volume that we thought were representative of that essay in some way. The second section contains suggestions that were submitted by PEP network members. In both cases, we could not include all the excellent citations that the annotated bibliography now contains. The development of the annotated bibliography is being overseen by Kareem Rabie, Max Ajl, and Omar S. Dahi. We owe a special thanks to Raymond Caraher and Tomer Stern who spent many hours annotating most of the citations you read below and many others not included.

Section 1: Selected Annotations from Essays

Submitter: Omar Dahi

Hyman P. Minsky, "The financial instability hypothesis: an interpretation of Keynes and an alternative to "standard" theory," *Challenge: The Magazine of Economic Affairs* 20, no.1 (1977), 20–27.

In this piece, Minsky constructs a theory for a "financially sophisticated" capitalist economy which shows why such an economy is inherently unstable. By focusing on an interpretation of Keynes derived from a rebuttal of his "classical" critics, Minsky demonstrates that his theory is both consistent with the *General Theory*, as well as better suited to explain our economy than the "standard" theory of the neoclassical synthesis. Instead of focusing on the rational, utility maximizing individuals of the "village fair paradigm," Minsky puts uncertainty of the future at the heart of his analysis. This radical—but realistic—uncertainty coupled with increasingly risky debt-financing makes stable growth impossible. During boom times, "a period in which the economy is doing well, views about acceptable debt structure change. In the deal-making that goes on between banks, investment bankers, and businessmen, the acceptable amount of debt to use in financing various types of activity and positions increases." This in turn inspires further investment and riskier debt-structures. This pro-cyclical momentum represents the tendency of the financially advanced capitalist economy to transform a period of "doing well" into a "speculative investment boom," bound to bring an economy to the brink of crisis.

After suggesting that this systemic financial instability debunks the validity of the neoclassical synthesis, Minsky concludes that it is up to policy makers to constrain speculative finance in order to establish a "good financial society."

Raul Prebisch, "Commercial Policy in the Underdeveloped Countries," *American Economic Review* 49, no.2 (1959), 251.

This essay is a response to the standard argument for commercial policy in Latin America. Prebisch summarizes the conventional narrative as being "let the peripheral countries increase productivity in their primary activities through much-needed technical progress and thus expand their exports. Their rate of development will then be accelerated on sound basis." However, Prebisch argues, policies adopting this framework will never allow the underdeveloped world to bridge the income gap with the core countries for two main reasons. First, technical progress in primary commodity production will not generate enough employment within the underdeveloped world. Secondly, the income elasticity of demand for underdeveloped countries' primary commodities are consistently lower than for Northern manufactures. Thus, Prebisch argues, import substitution—defined as the "increase in the proportion of goods that is supplied from domestic sources"—provides the only mechanism through which disparities in foreign trade elasticities can be corrected. The author then justifies this policy on theoretical grounds, addressing critics of this policy, as well as outlining the main mechanisms through which it could generate development.

Stephen A. Marglin, "What Do Bosses Do? The Origins and Functions of Hierarchy in Capitalist Production," *Review of Radical Political Economics* 6, no. 2 (1974), 60–112.

Is hierarchical authority a necessity dictated by our level of technological advancement, or is it produced, reproduced, and legitimized by our social and economic institutions? Marglin argues that if the answer is the former, then "self-expression in work must at best be a luxury reserved for the very few regardless of social and economic organization." Worker alienation would be unavoidable, as the exogenously determined level of technology would be what imposed the hierarchy. In order to investigate these premises, Marglin discusses the circumstances which gave rise to the boss-worker hierarchy, and thus transferred control of the work process from the actual producer to the capitalist. He argues that the two major movements which deprived workers of their means of production—the development of the "minute division of labor characterized by the putting out system," and the "development of the centralized organization of the factory system"—were innovations designed to transfer a larger share of the "pie" from workers to capitalists. The "subsequent growth in the size of the pie" obscures the class interests fundamental to innovations in organization. Therefore, Marglin argues, the "social function of hierarchical work organization is not technological efficiency, but accumulation."

Submitter: Max Ajl

Jonathan Nitzan & Shimshon Bichler, *Capital as Power : A Study of Order and Creorder* (Milton Park, Abingdon, Oxon; New York, NY: Routledge, 2009).

In a departure from both mainstream economics and Marxist political economy, Nitzan and Bichler present a theory of capital removed from the imagined units of utils or abstract labor. They propose a theory that positions capital as the "symbolic representation of power." Drawing on Veblen's distinction between "industry" and "business," they argue that finance, rather than being "fictitious capital," is the *only* form of capital. Thus, "the firm's expected earnings and their associated risk perceptions represent neither the productivity of the owned artefacts nor the abstract labor socially necessary to produce them, but the power of a corporation's owners." Unlike Liberal ideology and Marxist political economy, which views the state and capital as distinct entities, Nitzan and Bichler suggest that the "legal-organizational" entities of the corporation and the institutional networks of the government are "part and parcel of the same encompassing mode of power." From this point of view, capitalists' relative earnings represent a process of differential accumulation whereby the size of earnings relative to other capitalists denotes greater relative power. They emphasize that their view of power extends beyond the economy and politics, and acts as "organizational power at large," encompassing ideology, culture, violence, gender, conflict, and beyond—bringing society under a totalizing "logic of capital."

Karl Kautsky, *The agrarian question: in two volumes* (London; Winchester, Mass.: Zwan Publications, 1988).

In this work, Kautsky presents a study on the impact of capital on peasant societies, and the role of peasants in socialist revolution. He emphasizes that peasant production, while not specific to any historical mode of production, must be placed within the framework of capitalist development. Discussing the impact of capital on class within peasant society, Kautsky suggests that the small farms of the peasantry provide a source of labor-power for large capitalist farms, and thus growth in the number of large farms both reduces the supply of labor-power while at the same time increasing the demand for it. This contradiction, according to him, ensures the survival of small farms and the peasantry. This relationship of subservience of the small farms is exacerbated by the highly exploitable nature of the peasants themselves, from whom surplus-value is intensely extracted. However, Kautsky argues that the survivability of the peasant plays little role in the revolution, as technological advancement will eventually render the peasant obsolete—under either capitalism or socialism. In the revolution, the peasantry would either be eliminated or marginalized to the point of numerical and political insignificance. Thus, Kautsky suggests that socialists should waste no time in mobilizing peasants for the revolution; peasants, as a conservative force, could prove to be counter-revolutionary, and even mobilize against the proletariat.

Sandra Halperin, *War and social change in modern Europe : the great transformation revisited* (Cambridge, UK; New York: Cambridge University Press, 2004).

In a critical re-evaluation of Polanyi's *The Great Transformation,* Halperin seeks to explain the changing social order in Europe from the nineteenth century through World War II and how it relates to modern day "globalization." While Halperin agrees with much of the spirit of *The Great Transformation*, she argues that Polanyi's account of European history brushed over hundreds of bloody wars and conflicts: most of them class struggles. What was called the "Hundred Years' Peace" of seemingly little war between European states was actually marked by incredible conflict, and Polanyi's failure to recognize this places his analysis within the current of liberal thought that equates high finance with peace. Halperin traces the implications of this omission to argue that because Polanyi ignored the role of these class struggles, he "assigns them no role in shaping the development and operation of the market system and its central institutions," and thus fails to capture the reality of how societal processes and relationships shape the actions of states. These bloody conflicts were only resolved through the establishment of social democracies and the relative shift of power towards *labor* in the post-war era, which according to Halperin created relative peace and stability. However, Halperin suggests that this class compromise is now in danger of being usurped at the hands of neoliberal globalization.

Submitter: Joel Beinin

Beshara Doumani, *Rediscovering Palestine: Merchants and Peasants in Jabal Nablus, 1700-1900* (Berkeley: University of California Press, 1995).

In an attempt to "write the inhabitants of Palestine into history," Doumani utilizes local sources such as Islamic court registers and family newspapers to uncover the social histories of the merchants and peasants in Jabal Nablus. This social history is told through the "social lives" of four commodities: textiles, cotton, olive oil, and soap. Referring to the linkages between economic, political, and cultural factors embedded within the production, consumption, and exchange of these commodities, the author emphasizes how the "stories" behind these commodities illuminates the political economy of both the regional urban-rural relation and the larger political economy of the Ottoman Empire. The trade networks created through the production and transportation of these goods connected Nablus with Egypt, Beirut, Damascus, and its surrounding rural regions. These networks, Doumani argues, allowed Jabal Nablus to be fused "into a single fabric and its inhabitants into a single social formation." Focusing on different time periods for each commodity, Doumani sheds light upon the "convoluted journey of Jabal Nablus from a semi-autonomous existence under the umbrella of Ottoman rule" to a region deeply integrated and interconnected locally, regionally, imperially, and internationally under the capitalist world economy. Without knowledge of the social and economic relationships under Ottoman rule, Doumani argues that current Palestinian political identity cannot be adequately understood.

Joel Beinin, *Workers and peasants in the modern Middle East* (Cambridge, UK; New York: Cambridge University Press, 2001).

In this subaltern history of the Middle East, which Beinin defines as the area formerly ruled by the Ottoman Empire, a narrative concerned with of the majority of the population—namely, working class and peasantry—is advanced. Tracing the conditions of these classes from the eighteenth century, the author suggests that the workers and peasants constrained—or in certain cases, enhanced—the "power of state builders, entrepreneurs, and elite intellectuals as production processes, consumption patterns, political and social institutions, associational patterns, gender relations, public and private practices, experiences, and consciousnesses were transformed." After starting his discussion with the peasantry as the Ottoman Empire attempted to cope with increasing global pressures in the eighteenth and nineteenth century, Beinin then examines the Tanzimat reforms of the Ottoman Empire: how they affected the common people, and how the interference of European powers extinguished the coexistence between religious sects in the region. The rise of class consciousness and working-class mobilization in the twentieth century is also analyzed, particularly with regards to the nationalist movements and that elites that sought to employ, and as Beinin suggests, subvert and subordinate the interests of the working class.

Joel Beinin & Zachary Lockman, *Workers on the Nile: nationalism, communism, Islam, and the Egyptian working class, 1882-1954* (Princeton, NJ: Princeton University Press, 1987).

Drawing from the records of workers themselves, Beinin and Lockman provide a sweeping account of Egyptian labor history from the end of the nineteenth century to the regime of Nasir. They are particularly concerned with the "dialectic of class and nation," or the forms of consciousness and actions taken by workers within the context of foreign domination and the "struggle for national independence." Placing Egypt within the context of dependent capitalist development, the authors seek to uncover the barriers to class-based organization and the extent to which they were overcome. Given the uneven development amongst Egypt's industries, class-consciousness and labor organizing remained concentrated in a handful of large sectors: specifically, those tied to the cotton industry, such as transport workers before the World War II and textile workers afterwards. The authors trace the rise of working class movements and the different political organizations that sought their support, arguing that their objectives were hampered in the 1950s through a "historical compromise" that ended with a capitulation of the workers movement to the paternalistic states' economic benefits. Instead of continued mobilization, the workers movement was absorbed into the state in a corporatist manner under the banner of "Arab socialism." The authors argue that while recognizing the legitimacy of class, Arab socialism restricted the autonomy of the workers, forcing them into a position of subordinance and quiescence within the Nasirist state.

Submitter: Firat Bozcali

Arjun Appadurai, *The Social life of things : commodities in cultural perspective* (Cambridge Cambridgeshire; New York: Cambridge University Press, 1986).

This volume—comprised of essays written by historians, anthropologists, and an archaeologist—seeks to understand the "value" of commodities. These authors reject the neoclassical view that commodities are simply utility-providing objects traded in a neutral marketplace; they also go beyond the Marxist view that the labor time embodied in their production is the source of their value. The value of commodities are instead determined by their cultural and political meanings: the things themselves and the acts of exchange. The essays cover periods ranging from prehistoric Europe to twentieth-century India, and address topics related to commemoration and value, consumption and display, production regimes, and the anthropology of things.

Henri Lefebvre, *The production of space* (Malden, Mass.; Oxford, OX, UK: Blackwell, 1991).

With a Marxist framework, Lefebvre argues that space must be understood as the reproduction of social relationships, and discusses various constructions and manifestations of space. Reflecting on how space was created throughout history, particularly through the creation of the center-periphery divide, Lefebvre argues that shifts in the mode of production entails the production of a new space; thus, modern spaces reflect the current mode of production. Lefebvre also focuses on the triad of "perceived," "conceived," and "lived" space. Perceived space is where social life unfolds—ignored by the "conceived space" of urban planners and land speculators. The balance between these two spaces, Lefebvre argues, must leave room for a "lived space," where imagination through the arts and literature is preserved. Additionally, Lefebvre discusses the specialization of space, in which space is fragmented according to profession; dominated space, where space is transformed and mediated through technology; and abstract space—the realm of capitalism and commodities. Lefebvre concludes by discussing differential space as the counter to abstract space, which allows for challenges to the spatial norm and reflects what "socialism ought to be."

J.K. Gibson-Graham, *The End Of Capitalism (As We Knew It): A Feminist Critique of Political Economy* (Minneapolis: University of Minnesota Press, 2006).

This book seeks to challenge how the Left conceives of capitalism, and breaks with the Marxist tradition of conceptualizing class as universal categories engaged in struggle. Drawing from a wide range of critical theories, such as feminist theory, queer theory, and postmodern Marxism, Gibson-Graham argue that there is in reality a diverse set of exploitations and classes, and that the danger of conceptualizing capitalism as a singular, monolithic unity "discourages projects to create alternative economic institutions and class relations." They discuss the role of "alternative" economies, and highlight the potentially transformative aspects of household production, self-employment, and cooperatives. Framed around a discourse of "globalization," the authors suggest that the spread of capitalist culture—alongside the Left's conception of capitalism—is suffocating non-capitalist relations and pushing them further to the margins. By re-framing how capitalism is discussed, and suggesting that the non-capitalist modes of production that do exist be brought from the margins to the main stage, they fracture capitalism and "make its unity a fantasy."

Submitter: Melani Cammett

Karl Polanyi, *The Great Transformation: the political and economic origins of our time* (Boston, MA: Beacon Press, 2001).

In this critique of market liberalism, Polanyi seeks to answer why the hundred years' war gave way to world war, economic collapse, and ultimately the rise of fascism. By historically tracing the trajectory of these events, Polanyi argues that during the English industrial revolution, elites responded to the disruptions brought about by industrialization and emergent capitalism by developing the theories of market liberalism. England's position in the world economy allowed them to spread these ideas until they became the dominant doctrine of global capitalism. Society's response to this ideology—the second part of the "Double Movement," or the attempt to protect itself from the free market—generated tensions which inevitably led to the calamities of the twentieth century. Socialism and fascism are manifestations of the Double Movement, which is fundamentally a struggle over the "embeddedness" of the economy. Before the industrial revolution, Polanyi notes that in every society the economy was embedded within a larger framework of social relations. While there have always been markets, modern attempts to *disembed* it are what sets our market economy apart from everything that came before. A fully disembedded, self-regulating market society, Polanyi suggests, would "not exist for any length of time without annihilating the human and natural substance of society."

Kiren A. Chaudhry, "The myths of the market and the common history of late developers," *Politics & Society* 3 (1993), 245.

Chaudhry argues that the "new orthodoxy" of development economics—the neoliberal prescription of "state shrinking," "liberalization," and other free market reforms—is a misguided attempt to impose the seemingly neutral entity of "the market" upon states that have previously engaged in state-led development. Firstly, Chaudhry argues that the "neoliberal-liberal" construct of the market "rests on an abstract, stylized view of what market economies are and where they came from." Thus, the new orthodoxy cannot respond to the failure of late developers to create national markets. State and market-building are, according to Chaudhry, "mutually dependent and potentially conflicting processes," shaped by domestic and international historical circumstances, which are embedded within political interests and conflicts. Secondly, citing the dramatic change in capital flows between the 1970s and 1980s, Chaudhry argues that the new orthodoxy fails to recognize the role that changes in the international economy play in shaping the policies of late developers. To address the obstacles facing late developers, policy makers, and economists must recognize that "the market embodies no telos and has no self-contained blueprint on how societies should reconcile conflicts between individual and public goods."

Lily L. Tsai, *Accountability without democracy: solidary groups and public goods provision in rural China* (New York: Cambridge University Press, 2007).

Addressing the wide variations in the provisioning of public goods in China with the same formal systems and networks, Tsai proposes a counter to the typical narratives of unequal distribution, such as the level of economic development, or degree of democratic legitimacy. Using extensive data collected through a field study in over three hundred villages and four provinces, Tsai suggests that the existence of encompassing and embedded solidary groups capable of rewarding competent local officials with high moral standing is what determines the distribution of public goods. A solidarity group will improve the supply of public goods if "membership is based on shared moral obligations and ethical standards." The implications of this work propose that focusing solely on the rule of law will cause policy makers and social scientists to overlook existing "pockets of good governance in the absence of strong formal institutions."

Submitter: Wael Gamal

Thomas Piketty & Arthur Goldhammer, *Capital in the twenty-first century* (Cambridge Massachusetts: The Belknap Press of Harvard University Press, 2014).

Using data from the eighteenth to the twenty-first century, Piketty presents how wealth and income inequality has evolved throughout the developed world. Grounded in empirical rather than theoretical analysis, Piketty explains changing levels of inequality with a simple economic relationship, which is in turn explained by institutional and historical factors. If the difference between the average rate of return on capital (r) and (g) economic growth is large, than the share of national income going to capital will also be large, if not increasing. In other words, if the rate of return of capital remains significantly above the growth rate, "then the risk of divergence in the distribution of wealth is very high." In agrarian societies, as well as in Europe up until the world wars, inequality was massive, along with the gap between r and g. This changed after the massive destruction of capital during the world wars and the introduction of New Deal and welfare-state policies that introduced more progressive taxation measures. Piketty also discusses potentially convergent factors that can slow or reverse economic inequality, such as the diffusion of skills or knowledge. While acknowledging the political power of the super-wealthy, the author suggests that a possible response to increasing economic inequality would be a progressive global tax implemented by international institutions.

Submitter: Bassam Haddad

Adam Hanieh, *Capitalism and class in the Gulf Arab states* (New York: Palgrave Macmillan, 2011).

While recognizing some insights gained from the rentier state model, Hanieh largely breaks with that approach in order to better understand the position of the Gulf Cooperation Council within the global economy. By analyzing the development of capitalism in the Gulf Arab states through the 2008 crisis, Hanieh seeks to reveal the "untold story of the Gulf," or the reality of the region's development beyond the typical image of them as "monarchies sitting atop an oil spigot." Key to the author's analysis is the recent internationalization of Gulf conglomerates beyond their national boundaries to the rest of the Gulf countries, which reveals a "new set of internationalized social relations," and thus a process of class formation. This "Khaleeji" capitalist class reflects a process of reorientation of Gulf capital, centered around the "Saudi-UAE axis," and illuminates aspects of the political economy of the Gulf, the larger Middle East, and the world capitalist system as a whole. Hanieh argues that the Gulf states play a central role in the world economy as a major exporter of oil and provider of petrodollars—a cornerstone in the "adjustment of global economic imbalances." This central position is used to explain the Gulf's reliance on easily exploitable migrant laborers and highlight the threat that a labor movement in the Gulf could have on *global* capital accumulation.

Bassam Haddad, *Business networks in Syria : the political economy of authoritarian resilience* (Stanford, CA: Stanford University Press, 2012).

This study seeks to explain Syria's economic stagnation in one of "the most durable authoritarian regimes in the Middle East and the developing world." After the Ba'th party coup in the 1970s, the state began to dismantle the command economy and seek new methods of capital accumulation. However, the state elites did not want the national capitalist class to be able to challenge them politically, as political and ethnic tensions between the "rural-minoritarian" and "urban business class" created divisions among the parties. Haddad argues that the state instead established an informal state-business network characterized by mistrust and corruption. Waves of market liberalization in the 1980s and 1990s would serve to strengthen these networks and destroy any meaningful distinction between the public and private sectors. The combination of the clientelistic nature of the network and the absence of checks on the regime's power led to costly development outcomes, the end result being "unbridled and unproductive rent-seeking that produced egregious misallocation of resources."

Bassam Haddad, "Syria's State Bourgeoisie: An Organic Backbone for the Regime," *Middle East Critique* 21, no. 3 (2012), 231–257.

At the date this article was written, the Syrian regime had demonstrated remarkable "coherence and cohesion" since the start of the political turmoil. Attributing this resilience to the state bourgeoisie—the political elite "associated with the various institutions of the state as well as its ruling bodies"—this article examines the origins, composition, and aspects of this group in order to understand "one of the pillars of the Syrian regime's stability." Haddad also discusses the relationship between the state bourgeoisie and the rest of the private business class, arguing that while both groups are engaged in deeply-engrained networks that have yielded beneficial economic and political arrangements, different degrees of commitment of the private business class to the regime imply some threshold point where the loyalty of this class to the regime will be tested. This intra-elite breaking point suggests that while powerful, the backbone of the Syrian regime is not invincible.

David McNally, "The dialectics of unity and difference in the constitution of wage-labor: on internal relations and working-class formation," *Capital & Class* 1 (2015), 131.

In this article, McNally seeks to dialecticise the debate surrounding the politics of class and the politics of identity, reframing the discourses of race, gender, class, and sexuality—among other identities—to be understood as "internally constitutive of class." McNally also suggests that a pre-dialectical discourse between identity and class is indicative of a de-radicalized moment, and that the "universalism of bad class politics is simply the dialectical double of the bad (abstract) particularism of personal-identity theorists." Using insights from Hegalian-Marxist thought, the author recognizes the inter-constitution of the one and the many that "makes possible the concrete universality of wage-labor as a class." McNally argues that by "stripping 'class' of the multiple determinations which it is composed," the category itself is rendered empty. Therefore, working-class movements must develop a vision that recognizes how "differentiated social relations and forms come into being and through each other;" workers of all identities must self-consciously determine their own working class definitions. Such a working class politics, McNally argues, is in line with Fanon's "new humanism" and Marx's understanding of working-class self-emancipation.

Timothy Mitchell, *Rule of Experts: Egypt, techno-politics, modernity* (Berkeley: University of California Press, 2002).

In this book, Mitchell provides a narrative of Egypt's development in order to critique the idea of "modernization" in the underdeveloped world and the belief that Western experiences with technology can be imposed on the Global South. Grounded in a postcolonial context, this critique is expanded to encompass the concept of "the economy" and calls into question its existence as a "self-contained structure or mechanism whose internal parts are imagined to move in a dynamic and regular interaction, separate from the irregular interaction of the mechanism as a whole with what could now be called its exterior." Mitchell generates his argument by examining several major transformations undergone by Egypt in the twentieth century, such as the major construction project which changed the flow of the Nile, the use of chemicals, the spread of malaria, and the escalation of mechanized warfare. The author reveals several themes which have dominated Egypt's development, primarily "the character of calculability," forms of human agency, understandings of violence, and the politics of techo-science behind modern expertise.

Submitter: Aaron Jakes

Aaron Jakes, "A new materialism? Globalization and technology in the age of Empire," *International Journal of Middle East Studies* 47, no. ii (2015), 369–381.

In a rejection of contemporary notions of "globalization" epitomized by Friedman's *The World is Flat,* Jakes reviews five works that reconsider how technology impacted the Global South. Arnold's *Everyday Technology: Machines and the Making of India's Modernity* discusses the role of simple technology on the lives of everyday Indians. Barak's *On Time: Technology and Temporality in Modern Egypt* argues that the material makeup of technologies were not assembled prior to meaning being assigned to those objects. Gelvin and Green propose that globalization was predicated by critical globalizing events and the technologies associated with them. Huber, in *Channeling Mobilities: Migration and Globalization in the Suez Canal Region,* examines how globalization can be understood through the history of a global locality—in this case, the Suez Canal. The last work discussed by Jakes, Shamir's *Current Flow: The Electrification of Palestine* shows how the electrical grid's expansion through Palestine played an active role in accentuating the ethno-national divisions and tensions that have come to define the region. Through this literature review, Jakes identifies a "new materialism," with considerable differences from Marxist historical materialism. According to Jakes, while this "new materialism" does not disregard capital altogether, it does "actively refute the explanatory force of capitalist social relations while assigning historical agency to nonhuman objects." While recognizing theoretical issues related to this new materialism, Jakes suggests these works "invite us to reconsider the contours of Middle Eastern studies itself."

Sven Beckert, *Empire of cotton: a global history* (New York : Alfred A. Knopf, 2014).

By tracing the history of a single commodity—cotton—across history from the late pre-Columbian era to the eve of the twenty-first century, Beckert presents a "story of the making and remaking of global capitalism and with it the modern world." Beckert argues that the "great divergence" between the Global North and the rest of the world—a result of slavery, imperialism, and proletarianization—was only made possible through the unique characteristics required to produce and develop cotton: a commodity distinct from others, given its intensive labor needed from both fields and factories, alongside its scope as a global commodity. According to Beckert, cotton was the kindle for European "war capitalism" to spread across the world, and to shape and rearrange nation states, economies, and empire.

Submitter: Toby Jones

Toby C. Jones, *Desert kingdom: how oil and water forged modern Saudi Arabia* (Cambridge, Mass.: Harvard University Press, 2010).

In this book, Jones attempts to pry open the "black box" that is Saudi Arabia, which has remained on the margins of study due to various obstacles and closed doors. The author explores the connections between political power, expertise, oil, the environment, and Western technology, going beyond the standard framework of the rentier state and highlighting the importance of water and agriculture in the development of the Saudi state. Jones argues that modern Saudi Arabia, while an oil state, must also be viewed as a "technostate, one in which science and expertise, scientific services, and technical capacity came to define the relationship between the rulers and the ruled." The Western technology imported by the Saudi state-elite and the technical expertise that came with it gave the government the tools needed to exercise power, but also forced them into a relationship of dependence. With the underlying social inequalities and sectoral cleavages ignored, the Saudi government relies on this techno-political authority as its only source of legitimacy and credibility.

Submitter: Pete Moore

Anne M. Peters & Peter W. Moore, "Beyond Boom and Bust: External Rents, Durable Authoritarianism, and Institutional Adaptation in the Hashemite Kingdom of Jordan," *Studies in Compara-*

tive International Development (SCID) 3 (2009), 256.

Building upon and expanding rentier state theory, Moore and Peters seek to explain how "changes in external rent access and historically constituted demands on those rents" have forced the Hashemite Kingdom of Jordan to adapt. To maintain a cohesive regime coalition—based upon elites and Transjordanian tribes with changing demand for side payments—the monarchy has had to meet these demands by "modifying old distributional mechanisms and institutionalizing new venues," which take advantage of Jordan's geopolitically strategic position and the overall shifts in the international system's provisioning of rents. This "supply and demand" dynamic between those seeking side payments within the coalition and the regime which must supply them suggests further nuances within rentier state theory, which removes the image of a "static provision of rents by the international system as the sole explanatory variable for rentierism." Moore and Peters argue that the size of the regime coalition and geopolitical position are crucial determinants of the status of a rentier state, and that liberalization may more so act as a tool of coalition consolidation rather than a dispersion of power. By taking into account the historical dynamic of coalition demands on rents, the sources of rents, and the means through which distributive mechanisms are created, the authors suggest that rentier state theory can contribute to a wider understanding of authoritarian regime durability.

Pete Moore, "The bread revolutions of 2011: teaching political economies of the Middle East," *PS: Political Science & Politics* 2 (2013), 225.

In this piece, Moore suggests that political economy education is crucial for students attempting to grasp an understanding of the Arab uprisings of 2011, as well as for providing critical analytical techniques which can benefit students intellectually and academically. Moore focuses on two general political economy themes to clarify the lead-up to 2011: the politics of economic development, and resource politics. Highlighting the complex trajectories Middle Eastern countries took from state-led development to the era of neoliberal reform, Moore introduces ways in which American students will be uniquely situated to analyze change in this region of the world by connecting the bread revolutions with the Occupy Wall Street movement at home. Discussing oil in the Middle East, both within the rentier state paradigm as well as in the context of its geopolitical importance, Moore suggests that students can engage in material that will enhance and reframe their perspectives, and "counteract much of the popular media's fixation on violence, terrorism, and sectarianism." Through a variety of suggested assignments, students can grasp the tools and concepts needed to analyze change and resistance in societies, and appreciate the "struggles which shape states, regimes, and their citizens' voice."

Submitter: Mandy Turner

Hanna Batatu, *The old social classes and the revolutionary movements of Iraq: a study of Iraq's old landed and commercial classes and of its Communists, Ba'thists, and Free Officers* (London: Saqi Books, 2004).

Utilizing a substantial amount of socioeconomic data derived from unpublished sources and interviews, Batatu presents an analysis of society and the social classes of Iraq, outlining their role in history from the establishment of the nation-state to the time of writing. Tracing individual actors and events, Batatu presents a narrative of Iraq undergoing radical changes in its development as it was being brought under the realm of the capitalist world market. Batatu starts his narrative with the "old classes"—namely, the "upper landowners and the upper men of money and commerce"—which gained authority under the British mandate, and consolidated with the monarchy when faced with the threat of mass mobilization. Additionally, Batatu challenges the notion that class is "inapplicable to Arab societies," and seeks to determine "whether a class approach would open to view historical relations or social features that would otherwise remain beyond vision." In the later sections of the book, Batatu analyzes the Communists, Ba'thists, and Free Officers, in an effort to determine their motivations, social structures, successes, as well as the historical impact these movements had on the country.

Mandy Turner & Omar Schweiki, *Decolonizing Palestinian political economy: de-development and beyond* (Houndmills, Basingstoke, Hampshire; New York: Palgrave Macmillan, 2014).

Rejecting the dominant narrative that has divided Palestinians into separate and distinct groups, such Arab-Israeli, Bedouin, refugee, as well as other categories, and "reduced the Palestinian people to only those who reside within the occupied territory of the West Bank and Gaza," this collection seeks to reunite Palestinian political economy by reframing it into a single narrative. Starting with "de-development"—the "development" policies of the Israeli government in the occupied territories that have largely been pointed towards the goals of dispossession and disenfranchisement—this volume places the political economy of the Palestinian people at the "colonial matrix of dispossession, disenfranchisement, and destruction in a world-historical period regarded to be post-colonial." The book is divided into three sections—de-development explored, de-development applied, and de-development resisted—with contributions from fifteen authors with a wide range of backgrounds and fields. By challenging colonial narratives and analyzing the political economy of the Palestinian people as a whole, the authors seek to overturn the "disfigurement of history" that have marked previous accounts.

Submitter: Ahmad Shokr

Gilbert Achcar, *The people want: a radical exploration of the Arab uprising*, (Berkeley: University of California Press, 2013).

By taking a "radical" approach to understanding the Arab Uprisings of 2011, Achcar places the roots of the upheaval in the historical and economic circumstances that have hindered development in the region. Referring to Marx's theory that revolutions are sparked by tensions generated between the relations of production and the forces of production, the author argues that patrimonial and neo-patrimonial regimes, coupled with their status as rentier states, allowed crony capitalism, nepotism, and general corruption to dominate. This led to economic stagnation, and eventually frustrations reached a boiling point. However, Achcar suggests that these uprisings were not organized, and could not possibly overturn the deeply embedded regimes. Quoting Lenin at length,

and invoking the "Spring of Nations" and the French Revolution, Achcar argues that these tensions have created a "revolutionary situation" that could take decades to pay out. Therefore, Achcar argues that the "protracted or long-term revolutionary process" will not end until the tensions are addressed and replaced with a new social order.

John T. Chalcraft, *The striking cabbies of Cairo and other stories : crafts and guilds in Egypt, 1863-1914* (Albany: State University of New York Press, 2004).

Focused on crafts and service workers in Egypt from the early 1860s to World War I, Chalcraft examines how small-scale producers, manufacturers, and service providers lived, adapted, and "engaged in collective action during years of rabid world economic integration, state building, and colonial rule." Making heavy use of archival materials, this book breaks from typical histories "from below"—focused on workers who sell their labor-power to capitalists—and seeks to explore the resilience and restructuring of the artisans, cab drivers, tailors, weavers, and others who now make up the "informal sector." These professions are deeply tied to the Ottoman guilds, which the author argues were "transformed, co-opted, and increasingly disaggregated" as they resisted increasing European encroachment and attempted to adapt their institutions to the bureaucracies of the state. The weakening of the guilds, "alongside the lack of social legislation by the colonial state, helped accelerate and create forms of self-exploitation and labor squeezing." Coupled with new political realities, this resulted in protests which achieved some local victories, yet failed to substantially overhaul the conditions of crafts and service workers. This, alongside other social, economic, and political factors combined to create and perpetuate "a particular form of petty production and service provision in Egypt." The author concludes by rejecting the notion that there is a "universal or essential capitalism, for which various exceptions are made." Instead, Chalcraft proposes that "capitalism as a whole is heavily inflicted by political and social factors," and that these elements must be taken into account in order to understand the specific relations in question.

Submitter: Rafeef Ziadah

David McNally, Staple Theory as Commodity Fetishism: Marx, Innis and Canadian Political Economy, *Studies in Political Economy* 6, no. 1 (1981), 35–63.

In a criticism of Canadian political economy that integrates Innis's economic theory and Marx, McNally argues that "Staple Theory"—the Canadian experience of export-led development and its corresponding core-periphery relations—represents a form of "commodity fetishism," and more closely resembles the classical political economy of Adam Smith than that of Marx. Innis' work reflects a "'technicist' concept of production," which neglects the role of social relations behind the economy, and ignores that Marx argued all material relations are "socially mediated." As Marx's *Capital* is "a fundamental attempt to de-fetishize" relations within capitalist society, this attempt to integrate Innis and Marx leads to an irreconcilable contradiction. In its place, McNally suggests an analysis of Canadian political economy that supplants the "vulgar materialism" of Innis with a focus on class formation more representative of Marx's vision.

Himani Bannerji, *The dark side of the nation: essays on multiculturalism, nationalism and gender* (Toronto: Canadian Scholars' Press, 2000).

In these six essays, Bannerji takes a feminist-marxist and anti-racist perspective in order to criticize the mainstream discourse of "multiculturalism" in Canada. Focusing on the experiences of South Asian women and First Nations, Bannerji argues that Canadian policy has failed to address the actual concerns of racial minorities, and especially "non-white" women. Rather, multiculturalism's focus on diversity and difference ignores the economic, political, and social realities of racism, patriarchy, colonialism, and class, and abstracts from actual oppression. As long as the state rests on a legal system of private property, the multiculturalism of the state cannot truly alleviate the problems of racism, sexism, and other Marxist-feminist concerns. Placing the anglo-white male narrative of Canada within the larger context of the colonized world, Bannerji suggests that rather than a discourse of multiculturalism, a politics that centers resistance to oppression is necessary in order to form a liberatory agenda.

Submitter: Charles Anderson

Bayan N. al-Hout, "The Palestinian political elite during the Mandate period," *Journal of Palestine Studies* 9, no. i (1979), 85–111.

This investigation of the Palestinian elite during the mandate period presents the social, economic, and educational background of "one hundred political leaders and men holding responsible positions in political institutions." Pulling from interviews with either the individuals themselves, or close friends and family, al-Hout characterizes the Palestinian elite by three separate time periods: when leadership was either elected, a result of a party coalition, or appointed. He argues that the Palestinian elite was "more than a symbol." Rather, they represented "self-sacrificing leadership, and an example to the masses." However, the author notes that they failed to recognize the role of organized, mass political activity, and thus never articulated a politics of national resistance that was "something more than that of an instrument for the implementation of higher policy."

Zachary Lockman, *Comrades and enemies: Arab and Jewish workers in Palestine, 1906-1948* (Berkeley: University of California Press, 1996).

In a contribution to the social, political, and cultural history of modern Palestine and left-wing Zionism, the author challenges the framework of the "dual society paradigm": the notion that Arab and Jewish societies operated and evolved independently. Drawing on Arabic and Hebrew sources, this book explores the interactions between Arab and Jewish workers in Palestine during the British Mandate period. Emphasizing the voices and actions of the workers themselves, Lockman argues that Zionism and the Zionist movement was "shaped in crucial ways by their interactions with the Arab society they encountered." Focusing on labor Zionism and its interactions with Palestine's Arab working class, Lockman provides a narrative which reveals the complex history behind the labor Zionists' efforts to organize Palestinian workers, as well as its "largely unknown record of its relations with Arab workers and the Arab labor movement." Specifically, the author tells the story of the Arabs and Jews who worked on Palestine's railways, whose complex relationships reveal the "interactive and mutually formative" influence the workers—as well as their corresponding movements—had on each other.

Section 2: Selected Annotations from Members

Submitter: Julia Elyachar

Julia Elyachar, "Rethinking Anthropology of Neoliberalism in the Middle East," *Companion to the Anthropology of the Middle East* (2015), 411.

In this article, Elyachar attempts to reframe the anthropology of neoliberalism in the Middle East within the context of the violence and upheavals that have marked the region for over a decade. Elyachar argues that rather than being an exceptional case, the Middle East has acted as the "crucible of change" for a neoliberalism distinguished by its links to violence. Turning to the classical political economy of Adam Smith, Elyachar emphasizes the importance of the region to the development of political economy thought, before discussing how the concept of "development" laid the groundwork for neoliberalism in the Middle East. Elyachar then draws on the Calculation Debates of the twentieth century and turns to the formulations and politics of the theory and movement "calling itself neoliberal" to emphasize that the discourse of neoliberalism must be placed within the larger context of "the market society" and its limits. Elyachar concludes by emphasizing that the "link between markets and blood" is an ever present theme, and that to understand neoliberalism in the Middle East it is essential to utilize anthropology alongside political economy.

Julia Elyachar, "Upending Infrastructure: Tamarod, Resistance, and Agency after the January 25th Revolution in Egypt," *History & Anthropology* 25, no.4 (2014), 452-471.

Drawing from an ethnography conducted in Egypt after the January 25 Revolution and the election of President Morsi, Elyachar examines the "relation between massive revolt, infrastructure, and social theory." Centering the analysis on the mass mobilization movement *Tamarod*—a leading actor in calling for Morsi to step down—the author argues that *Tamarod* illuminated and upended "a social infrastructure of communicative channels in Egypt." By channels, Elyachar refers to a broad category of resources which relate a signer to an interpreter and form distinct objects themselves as "sets of infrastructure." Additionally, Elyachar reframes the discourse on agency and resistance in the Middle East, emphasizing its "distributed, dialogic, and historically constituted" aspects. This demonstrates agency's embeddedness within infrastructure, which is then upended during uprisings. Elyachar concludes by questioning the role of social theory and the position of the social scientist in "the apparent permanency of a prolonged impermanence," highlighting the necessity of finding "new indices of resistance."

Submitter: Arang Keshavarzian

Arang Keshavarzian, *Bazaar and state in Iran : the politics of the Tehran marketplace*, (Cambridge, UK ; New York : Cambridge University Press, 2007).

Keshavarzian compares the position of the Iranian Bazaar under the Shah with their position within the Islamic Republic from 1979 to the present. While the Shah implemented modernization policies that excluded the Bazaar, they were able to maintain their autonomy and survive. The Islamic Republic sought to "preserve the Bazaar," which contrarily restructured and weakened the institutions central to the Bazaar's operation. Seeking to explain this contradiction, the author argues that during the Shah's regime, the downgrading of the Bazaar resulted in autonomy and a "concentration of commercial value chains within the physical confines of the marketplace." This allowed for cooperative hierarchies and solidarity despite differences in power and status. However, the Islamic Republic's regime—marked by a "complex matrix of objectives and agendas"—co-opted, regulated, and replaced the commercial value chains, creating a "coercive hierarchy," diminishing collective solidarity and limiting its ability to mobilize. By focusing on the transition of the Iranian Bazaar from cooperative to coercive, Keshavarzian shows how state institutions and policies cleave and uproot social relations—in this case, undermining the elites' own agenda.

Ellis Goldberg, *Tinker, tailor, and textile worker: class and politics in Egypt, 1930-1952* (Berkeley: University of California Press, 1986).

Drawing on Egyptian, French, and British sources, Goldberg presents a narrative of Egyptian workers that focuses on the "relation between work and politics" and the "politics of an emerging working class." The author explores the dynamic between competing ideologies of mass mobilization—communism, nationalism, and Islam—and the actual ways in which the workers themselves organized. Goldberg analyzes the workers and organizing of five different Egyptian industries—craft production, sugar mills, oil refining, tobacco manufacturing, and textiles—to illuminate how these ideologies are reflected in the decisions of workers. Goldberg argues that the particular economic contexts of each industry explains the workers' political orientation; given this framework, the text illuminates why oil workers mobilized under nationalist elites, while textile workers formed a Leninist trade union, and sugar mill workers backed the Muslim Brotherhood.

Submitter: Aaron Jakes

George Henderson, *California & the fictions of capital* (New York: Oxford University Press, 1999).

Starting with the premise that California's economic and cultural development is entwined by "the alchemy of capital and nature," Henderson presents an interdisciplinary work of historical geography, political economy, and literary criticism to show that California's development in the late nineteenth and early twentieth century is structured by the "uneasy relations between capitalism and agriculture." Henderson begins his narrative at the end of the California gold rush, where the literal "unity of money and nature" was disturbed, and explains how the desire to maintain this unity was transplanted onto agriculture. However, Henderson suggests this bourgeois ambition was not easily perpetuated. Given that agriculture "embodies capital and simultaneously resists it," Henderson explores the implications of this contradictory character both for California's capitalist development, as well as for "bourgeois

cultural production"—processes interwoven into a single political economy. Framing both processes under the phenomenon of uneven development, distinguished by its temporal, social, and spatial aspects, the author argues that the Californian "rural realism" novels were efforts at "theorizing bourgeois economy in ways sympathetic to bourgeois anxieties." By both expressing bourgeois concern over the unity of capital and agriculture and encouraging urban investment into the rural setting, the "California Novel" helped resolve the dilemmas in organizing capitalist production in agriculture.

Jason W. Moore, "Transcending the Metabolic Rift: a theory of crises in the capitalist world-ecology," *The Journal of Peasant Studies* 1 (2011).

Starting from the critical political ecology theory of metabolic rift, Moore seeks to transcend the Cartesian binary of accumulation crises and ecological crises and "move towards a theory of crisis and development that views the accumulation of capital, the pursuit of capital, and the production of nature as differentiated moments within the singularity of historical capitalism." Rather than *having* an ecological regime, the author insists that capitalism *is* an ecological regime. Moore critiques the position of nature and society within metabolic rift theory: as binary, and the result of a confused dialectical relation between these two concepts. Moore then builds upon metabolic rift theory, arguing that it does not go far enough. Drawing upon Marx's theory of value, as well as the dialectic of underproduction and overproduction at the core of Marx's theory of crisis, the author proposes a theory of "capitalism as world-ecology." This perspective unifies the processes of capitalist development and crisis, and insists that rather than acting upon nature, capitalism develops through "nature-society relations." Capitalism as world-ecology offers a new way of conceptualizing the metabolic rift, and positions the current neoliberal era not only as a possible turning point in historical capitalism, but also as an "epochal ecological crisis."

Submitter: Raymond Hinnebusch

Alex Callinicos, *Imperialism and global political economy* (Cambridge, UK; Malden, MA: Polity Press, 2009).

Beginning with the assertion that "empire is back with a vengeance," Callinicos seeks to "liberate the theory of imperialism" from the limitations of its classical forms. The book starts with a critical review of the classical Marxist theories of imperialism: Lenin, Bukharin, Luxemburg, among others, as a means of developing his own theory. Critiquing these theories for putting financial capital at the core of imperialism, Callinicos instead argues that imperialism is best understood at the intersections under two competitive logics: the logic of accumulation and the logic of geopolitics. This formulation of imperialism, Callinicos argues, allows for a theory that is historically open, non-reductionist, and reflective of the operations of capitalism within the core-periphery framework. The author then lays out a history of imperialism under the lens of this framework, broken up into three time periods: classical imperialism (1870-1945), superpower imperialism (1945-1991), and imperialism after the Cold War (1991-). Falling within the radical socialist tradition, Callinicos recognizes the systemic roots of empire lie within capitalism; a change in hegemon is merely a "change of masters."

Raymond Hinnebusch, "The Middle East in the world hierarchy: imperialism and resistance," *Journal of International Relations & Development* 14, no. 2 (2011), 213.

This article attempts to analyze and identify the position of the Middle East within the world hierarchy: one of exceptional subordination, yet remarkably resistant to its dominance. The author engages in a survey of the region, from its peripheralization and fragmentation to the emergence of its clientalist hierarchy, foreign policy, rebellions, and continued struggle with global hegemons. With a Marxist-inspired structuralist framework which embraces dependency theory and world systems theory, Hinnebusch seeks to "upgrade" structuralism to incorporate identity, polarity, and anarchy—variables considered in rival international relations theories—in order to more powerfully explain the international politics of the Middle East region. Hinnebusch argues that this upgraded structuralism allows for the crucial centering of imperialism—an aspect ignored in other theories—in exposing the origins of the regional system, as well as in explaining the roots of ongoing instability in the Middle East. The incorporation of these variables, Hinnebusch suggests, allows structuralism to both strike "a better balance between structure and agency" than its rivals, as well as enhance the explanatory power of structuralism itself and overcome its critiques.

Submitter: Shir Hever

Neve Gordon, "The Political Economy of Israel's Homeland Security," *The Surveillance Project*, (n.d.).

In this article, Gordon seeks to explain the incredible popularity and perceived success of Israel's homeland security industry in the years following 9/11. Drawing an analogy to the "experience economy"—the commodification of experience—the author argues that the experiences of Israel itself, such as its history with suicide bombers, has played a crucial role in shaping the industry, as well as its perception abroad as a "global success story." After positioning the Israeli homeland security industry within the Israeli economy and the international surveillance industry, Gordon discusses the historical process which led to the emergence of Israel's homeland security industry within the context of the military and technology industries. The author argues that the success of the industry generates an economic incentive to "produce and reproduce the so-called security-related experiences and to diversify them." The desirability of Israel's homeland security industry is further enhanced by its ability to construct this industry alongside a neoliberal economic agenda in line with perceived democratic values.

Shir Hever, *The Political Economy of Israel's Occupation : Repression Beyond Exploitation*, (London ; New York, NY : Pluto, 2010).

Beginning with a cost-benefit analysis of the Israeli occupation, Hever argues that the costs of the occupation—with the exception of a handful of industries—largely outweigh the benefits, and that this loss is expected to increase over time. Hever then suggests that economic exploitation cannot fully explain the occupation due to the exclusion of Palestinians from the Israeli labor force and the rising costs experienced by the state. Seeking to explore this seemingly contradictory outcome, the author goes beyond Marxist theory to incorporate works and concepts from Bourdieu and from institutional political economy, criticizing the "Israeli Anomaly" theory: the phenomenon of the Jewish-Israeli working class voting against their interests and continuing to support the occupation, despite its detrimental effects on society. The author argues that Jews receive "social capital" over non-Jews, positioning them higher within the social hierarchy, and inspiring further perpetuation of the occupation. Turning to the possibility of resolution, the author discusses two possible scenarios for how the resistance and oppression dynamics may reach two different outcomes.

Submitter: Sherene Seikaly

Catherine Gallagher, *The body economic: life, death, and sensation in political economy and the Victorian novel* (Princeton, NJ: Princeton University Press, 2006).

This book is an intellectual history of nineteenth-century Britain. It shows how political economists and writers had shared assumptions. For example, labor was, in Victorian times, supposed to make you miserable; people like Charles Dickens went out of their way to show that their authorial labor was bona fide work that makes one as authentically miserable as any other kind of labor. Labor ought to make you miserable, or it is not authentic. Gallagher discusses at length the novel *Hard Times* and its "notorious lack of play," and suggests that the Romantics shared some premises with the political economists they assaulted. However, there was a gap between these premises and those of the early Victorians; earlier eudemonism was abandoned. *Hard Times* does not gainsay productivism—a focus of the Victorians—but it is stuck between wanting to "acknowledge importance of happiness and being unable to imagine how it might proceed from work." Thus, Victorians measured virtue by the capacity to produce. The cult of work and how labor functions for writers like George Eliot is an "antiseptic." Thus the laboring author for George Eliot "is also compensated for her pains by a satisfying consciousness for moral superiority."

Susan Buck-Morss, "Envisioning Capital: Political Economy on Display," *Critical Inquiry* no. 2 (1995), 434.

In this piece Buck-Morss explains how the liberal-democratic tradition does not rest on the political notion of nationalism but rather on an economic notion of a collective based on the depersonalized exchange of goods. She describes how the framing of the economy was coterminous with capitalism, thus the description of one entailed the description of the other. She explores how Michel Foucault and the neo-Kantians before him have long shown how science creates its object. She also points out that the motive force of Adam Smith's understanding of economy was not instrumentally and rationally calculated demand but rather desire. Buck-Morss also makes the crucial point that "the conception of the progress of civilization as the unlimited increase of objects produced for sale was a defining moment of modernity." Finally, she points out that Marx's insistence that the human effects of the economy be made visible and palpable remains his contribution to political economy.

Submitter: Firat Demir

Adam Smith, *The theory of moral sentiments* (Mineola, NY: Dover Publications, 2006).

In this predecessor to his magnum opus, Smith seeks to understand and explain moral practices. Building on Hume, Smith rejects the "state of nature" as prerequisite for the creation of civil society, and suggests that morality represents an adaptation to humanity's circumstances. Distinguishing between the "negative" virtue of justice and the "positive" virtue of benevolence, Smith suggests that because of the individuality and uncertainty of human life, it is not possible to generate a "universal" good. He formulates a theory encompassing the seemingly contradictory aspects of human nature marked by self-interest in one moment, and sympathy the next.

Andre G. Frank, *ReOrient: global economy in the Asian Age*, (Berkeley: University of California Press, 1998).

By turning Eurocentric historiography and social theory upside down, and advocating for a "globological" perspective, Frank presents a narrative of the world economy from 1400-1800 that deconstructs the anti-historical ideology behind the "rise of the West." The author confronts Eurocentric paradigms—replacing them with "humanocentric ones"—to argue that if there was a "centre" economy during this time, it was in Asia; Europe's domination is a more recent phenomenon. Rejecting typical arguments that explain European hegemony, Frank argues that American money allowed Europe to "muscle in on and benefit from Asian production, markets and trade," profiting from Asia's position as the dominant power. Europe "climbed up on the back of Asia, then stood on its shoulders," giving it a temporary position as the global leader. Development, Frank suggests, was not "of the West," but of the world economy as a whole. Within the context of this world historical perspective, the development of East Asia fails to fit into the schema of misconceived, Eurocentric theories of development celebrating the "magic of the market." Fitting into a "global economic development scheme," the apparent "rise of East Asia" merely represents another "transplant" of dominance—from "the West," to where it departed only two centuries ago.

Ellen M. Wood, *The origin of capitalism: a longer view*, (London: Verso, 2002).

Rejecting the notion that capitalism represents some fruition of humanity's innate qualities, Wood presents a narrative of the origins of capitalism removed from an ideology that positions capitalism as the "natural" destination of history. Critical of both mainstream and Marxist histories, Wood proposes that underlying these accounts is an assumption that capitalism has always existed in some form: in other words, "they have assumed the prior existence of capitalism in order to explain its coming into being." This "naturalization," Wood argues, denies the "specificity" of capitalist relations and forms, and buries "the long and painful historical process that brought it into being." Instead, Wood shifts the focus from the towns of European feudalism—typically posited as the "natural enemy that would destroy the feudal system"—to the countryside, centering the agrarian origin of capitalism. Tracing the evolution of social relations in seventeenth-century England, Wood argues that while elites on the continent continued to utilize "extra-economic" force to extract a surplus, the demilitarization of the lords

and the centralization of the English state resulted in "the complete dispossession of direct producers," who are "legally free and whose surplus labor is appropriated by purely 'economic' means." By detaching "capitalist from bourgeois" and "capitalism from the city," Wood addresses deeply held assumptions throughout Western culture, and undermines convictions about capitalism's compatibility with democracy and social justice.

John Locke, *Second treatise of government* (New York: Barnes & Noble Books, 2004).

Written to justify the reign of King William, Locke presents an argument which posits the sovereignty of the government as subordinate to the will of the majority. Beginning by discussing the "state of nature"—where natural law governs, and all are "free" and "equal"—Locke explains the origins of civil society as a means of protecting private property, of which absolute freedom offers no protection. Thus, Locke argues, people will form a commonwealth, under which they sacrifice natural freedoms and complete autonomy in order to gain the protection of government. However, when this government becomes subservient to some other force—either itself, or a foreign entity—and no longer represents the people, then it loses its justification to exist; people should revolt against it, as it has broken its "social contract" to the masses.

John M. Keynes, *The general theory of employment, interest and money* (New York: Harcourt, Brace, 1935).

Addressing his colleagues at a time when "the world will not much longer tolerate the unemployment" of the capitalist economy in crisis—the Great Depression—Keynes seeks to challenge the mainstream "classical theory" of the time, and "cure the disease" afflicting capitalism. Keynes presents a "study in the scale of output and employment as a whole" that radically differs from his contemporaries, arguing that "classical theory" is merely a special case which assumes characteristics that "happen not to be those of the economic society in which we actually live." In its place, Keynes provides a general theory, in which the propensity to consume, the schedule of the marginal efficiency of capital, and the rate of interest determine new investment—and in turn, the "increment of employment." Keynes's study of investment reveals that a monetary economy "is essentially one in which changing views about the future are capable of influencing the quantity of employment." From this, he suggests it is "unlikely that the influence of banking policy on the rate of interest will be sufficient by itself to determine an optimum rate of investment." Instead, Keynes proposes that a "somewhat comprehensive socialization of investment will prove the only means of securing an approximation to full employment." The book concludes by addressing the power that economic ideas have in the world, suggesting that "the ideas of economists and political philosophers, both when they are right and when they are wrong, are more powerful than is commonly understood. Indeed the world is ruled by little else."

Joseph A. Schumpeter, *Capitalism, socialism, and democracy* (London: Allen & Unwin, 1943).

Reflecting on forty years of "thought, observation, and research on the subject of socialism," Schumpeter tells the story of capitalism's "paradoxical conclusion"—how it will be "killed off by its achievements." After reviewing Marx from sociological, economical, and prophetic perspectives, Schumpeter outlines his own theory of "creative destruction": the process of entrepreneurs driving capital accumulation and growth at the expense of obsolete, unproductive firms. However, Schumpeter argues this process will gradually stall due to the increasing monopoly power of firms and their ability to resist entrepreneurial challenge. Suggesting that the line between monopoly power and central planning is blurred, Schumpeter argues that socialism—provided "that the requisite stage of industrial development has been reached" and "that transitional problems can be successfully resolved"—can work. After reviewing the classical theory of democracy, and proposing his own, Schumpeter evaluates the compatibility of socialism and democracy, arguing that there could exist a democratic socialism, but that "socialist democracy may turn out to be more of a sham than capitalist democracy ever was." In order to put the preceding sections of the book in perspective, Schumpeter concludes with a historical sketch of the major socialist parties of Western history. Discussing the possible trajectories of capitalism and socialism after the world wars, Schumpeter suggests that while socialism is predictable, "there is little reason to believe that this socialism will mean the advent of the civilization of which orthodox socialists dream."

Marshall Berman, *All that is solid melts into air: the experience of modernity* (New York: Viking Penguin, 1988).

Pulling from a range of political and literary writers, Berman presents a "study of the dialectics of modernization and modernism." At the heart of Berman's text are the seemingly endless paradoxes of modern life. While processes of scientific advancement, industrialization, state-building, mass communication, and mass mobilization—processes reflective of modernization—have reshaped the world, they have simultaneously inspired images and visions of the future which people seek to utilize to change the world *themselves*. It is from these contradictions that Berman continues his study, centering capitalism as the stage upon which modern society is based. Seeking to "bring the dynamic and dialectical modernism of the nineteenth century to life again," the author argues that the modernisms and modernists of the past—Goethe, Marx, Baudelaire, Petersburg, among others—can provide perspective on the current contradictions of modern life. Understanding their modernism, Berman suggests, is necessary to understand our own and to create the modernism of the future.

Max Weber & Stephen Kalberg, *The Protestant ethic and the spirit of capitalism* (Los Angeles: Roxbury Pub. Co., 2002).

Distinguishing a "modern" capitalism distinct from capitalist exchange present since antiquity, Weber seeks to locate the source of the "spirit of capitalism"—or the "ethically-oriented maxim for the organization of life"—inherent in modern Western society. Beginning his analysis with an investigation of the wealth inequality between Catholics and Protestants, Weber argues that "Protestants have demonstrated a specific tendency toward economic rationalism," and that this inequality must "mainly be sought in the enduring inner quality of these religions," rather than "only in their respective historical-political, external situations." Weber locates this ethic within ascetic Protestantism itself, suggesting that the Puritans placed systematic, methodical, and specialized work—

alongside striving for profit—above all else. This sanctification of labor provided a cultural stimulus which spurred the development of modern capitalism, and the phenomenon of industrialization that came along with it. Weber concludes by addressing the values of his own age, arguing that rather than needing a cultural incentive for labor, it has become the impetus itself.

Pierre-Joseph Proudhon & Pierre-Joseph Proudhon, *System of economical contradictions; or, The Philosophy of misery* (New York: Arno Press, 1972).

While affirming the utility of economics as a science, Proudhon rejects the political economy of Smith, Ricardo, and Say, exposing it as an apology for private property and wage-labor replete with "contradictory hypotheses and equivocal conclusions." In this book, Proudhon seeks to "unfold the system of economic contradictions" as a means of advocating for its conclusion; "to exhibit the genesis of the problems of production and distribution is to prepare the way for their solution." Uncovering these contradictions, Proudhon argues that within the division of labor is the tendency to "cause the multiplication of wealth and the skill of workers" yet simultaneously generate "intellectual degeneracy" and "continual, civilized misery," and the use of technology—distinguished by the characteristic of wage-labor—has further magnified this rift. Competition—thought of as an "inspiration of justice"—is, according to Proudhon, unjust. From monopoly power to police and taxation, Proudhon reveals additional contradictions at the heart of capitalism, reaffirming that the only means of transcending them is through its termination.

Vladimir I. Lenin, *Imperialism, the highest stage of capitalism : a popular outline* (Peking: Foreign Languages Press, 1965).

Written during the imperialist First World War, Lenin seeks to show how imperialism—"the monopoly stage of capitalism"—lays on the eve of socialist revolution. Capitalism, Lenin argues, had developed into a world system of "colonial oppression" and of the "financial strangulation of the overwhelming majority of the people" by few dominant countries. Lenin begins by describing how the rise of monopolies—a result of the concentration of production—is a fundamental law of capitalism. Monopolies encourage the merging of industrial capital with bank capital, which in turn creates a basis for finance capital, concentrating into a financial oligarchy. Lenin suggests that this transition from the dominance of "capital in general" to finance capital results in the "predominance of the entrepreneur" and a "crystallization" of a small number of financially powerful states, which instead of exporting goods, export capital. The desire to control all raw materials by the increasingly powerful monopolies expands with colonialism: capital accumulation on the world stage. As monopolies expand their "spheres of influence" and potential colonies become sparse, the only option for imperialist powers becomes redivision—a process marked by formal war and violence. However, Lenin argues that the era of finance capital is marked by a "state of decay." While monopolies enhance the contradictions of capital, they also represent a process of socializing the means of production. This signals that while imperialism "may continue in a state of decay for a fairly long period," it must eventually collapse.

[Bibliography submitted by Omar Dahi.]

Books from **Tadween**

A Life in Middle East Studies
Roger Owen

Coming Fall 2016

Roger Owen's academic and professional life has been spent teaching, studying, visiting, making friends and, in general, trying to understand the region via its politics, economic life, history and popular culture. He decided to keep an almost daily journal recording his thoughts and feelings, as well as being asked to write a regular op-ed column for the Arabic newspaper, *Al-Hayat* beginning in 1986. This memoir is an attempt to record and make sense of a life spent studying a culture very different from his own.

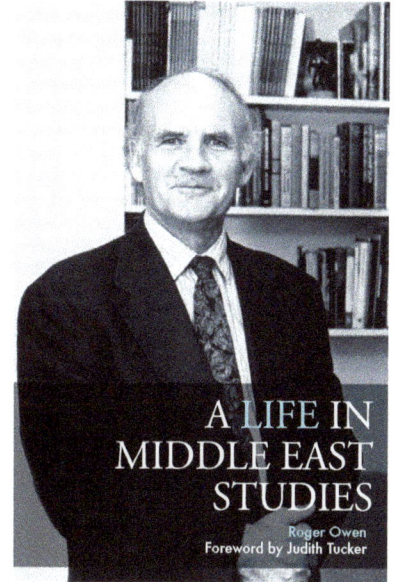

في ســوريا، تخفي الكثير من الحدائق جثث القتلى من الناشــطين، وتحمـي من بقي حيا منهم من الضربات العنيفة للنــظام. فـي تـلك الــحــدائـق تــحكي المــدافـن المــنزلية، ثمّـة تعاون تانيا الخـوري مســتــمر بين الأحياء والأموات. الأموات يحمـون الأحيـاء من خلال عـدم تعريضهم للمزيد مـن الخطـر علـى يـد الدولـة، والأحياء يرعـون أموانهـم ويحفظـون هوياتهم وقصصهم فـي باطـن الأرض، رافضين أن يتحوّل موتهـم جزءاً من أدوات النظام فـي التلاعـب بالتاريـخ. الحدائق تحكي هـو عـرض فنـي تفاعلـي يجـول العالـم، ليـروي التاريـخ الشــفوي لعشرة أشـخاص دفنوا فى حدائق سورية. رُكبت هذه الحكايـات بعناية مـع أصدقاء القتلى وأفراد أسـرهم، لنـروي قصصهم كما كانـوا ليرووها بأنفسـهم. يحتوي هذا الكتـاب علـى الروايات العشـر باللغتين الإنكليزيــة والعربية المحكية. مع مقدّمة للفنانة ورسـوم تصوّر تجربة العرض الحيّ.

Gardens Speak
Tania El Khoury

$14.99

Gardens Speak is an interactive sound installation that toured around the world. It contains the oral histories of ten ordinary people who were buried in Syrian gardens. This book contains the narrative text of those ten oral histories, which have been constructed in collaboration with the friends and family of the deceased, in both English and spoken Arabic. It includes an acknowledgement and introduction by the artist, and illustrations of the audience experience in *Gardens Speak*.

NGOs in the Arab World Post-Arab Uprisings
Noura Erakat & Nizar Saghieh

$9.99

In a unique collection of essays that covers the expanse of the Arab popular protest movements, *Mediating the Arab Uprisings* offers spirited contributions that elucidate the remarkable variation and context behind the fourth estate's engagement with these mass protests. These essays go beyond the cursory discussion to historicize media practice, unsettle pre-existing suppositions about the uprisings, puncture the pomposity of self-righteous expertise on the region, and shatter the naiveté that underlies the reporting of the uprisings.

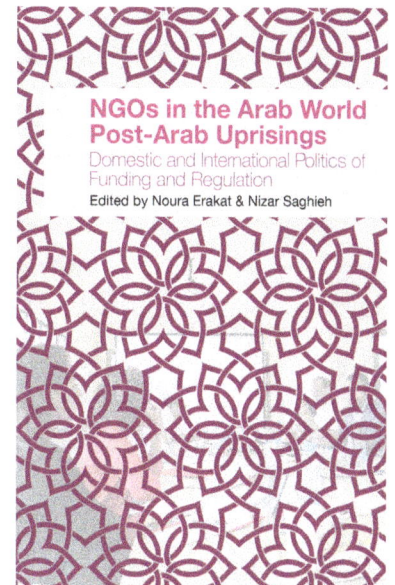

To purchase books, visit www.tadweenpublishing.com

Jil Oslo: Palestinian Hop Hop, Youth Culture, and the Youth Movement
Sunaina Maira

from $12.00

Based on ethnographic research conducted in Palestine, primarily during the Arab uprisings, this book explores the intersections between new youth cultures and protest politics among Palestinian youth in the West Bank and Israel. It focuses on Palestinian hip hop and the youth movement that emerged in 2011. Challenging the Oslo framework of national politics and of cultural expression, these young artists and activists are rethinking and reviving the possibility of a decolonial present.

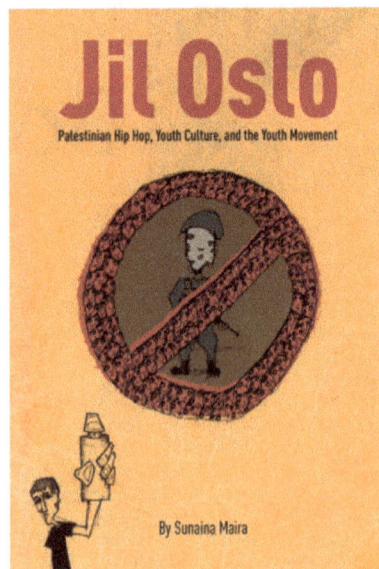

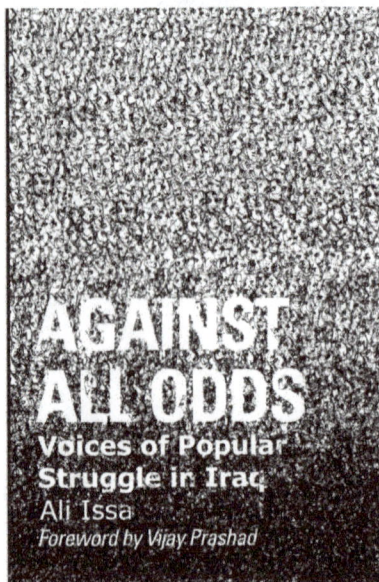

Against All Odds: Voices of Popular Struggle in Iraq
Ali Issa

from $8.99

Collected from dozens of interviews with, and reports from, Iraqi feminists, labor organizers, environmentalists, and protest movement leaders, *Against All Odds* presents the unique voices of progressive Iraqi organizing on the ground. Dating back to 2003, with an emphasis on the 2011 upsurge in mobilization and hope as well as the subsequent embattled years, these voices belong to Iraqis asserting themselves as agents against multiple local, regional, and global forces of oppression.

Critical Voices
Ziad Abu-Rish & Bassam Haddad

from $11.99

Comprised of twenty-seven interviews with leading researchers, intellectuals, artists, and activists, *Critical Voices* explores the ways in which power and popular mobilizations manifest in the contemporary region, as well as the representation of key dynamics, experiences, and figures. Through their own unique perspectives and possibilities, the interviewees and interviewers challenge the ways in which the region is studied, discussed, and represented.

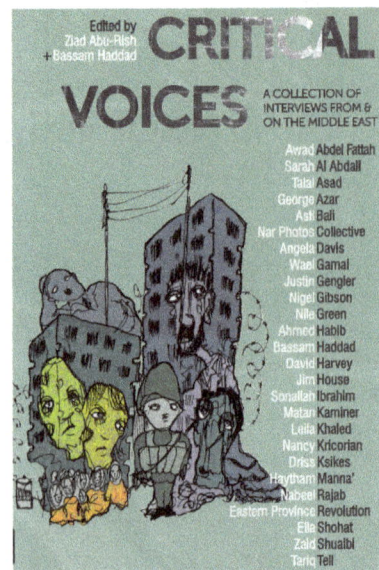

To purchase books, visit www.tadweenpublishing.com

JadMags from Tadween

Theorizing the Arabian Peninsula

Print copy $7.49
Electronic copy $4.99

Despite the sophisticated, critical, and oft-politically engaged literature emerging from and about the Arabian Peninsula, the region remains marginalized, in multiple ways, within academic and popular analyses. This JadMag addresses the ways in which frameworks of knowledge production have not only obscured social realities there, but also contributed to their construction. Our roundtable contributors approach this project from a number of different disciplinary perspectives and theoretical standpoints.

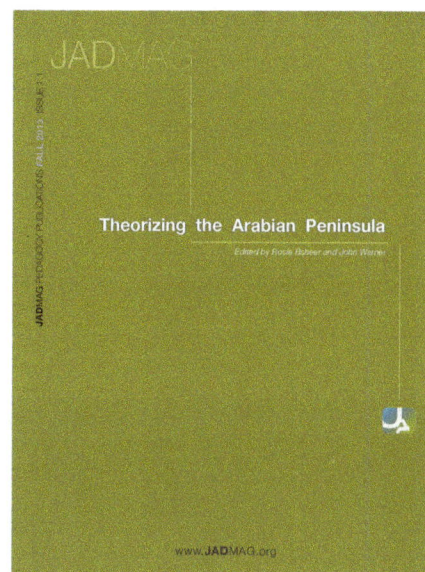

Beyond Dominant Narratives on the Western Sahara

Print copy $6.99
Electronic copy $3.99

Both media and academic scholarship have marginalized the Western Saharan conflict, rendering it largely insignificant within regional and global political imaginations. After decades of violence, tens of thousands of deaths and even more refugees, the territorial dispute over the Western Sahara remains unresolved and underreported. This pedagogical publication seeks to shift away from dominant narratives on the Western Saharan conflict and shed light on more nuanced views and approaches.

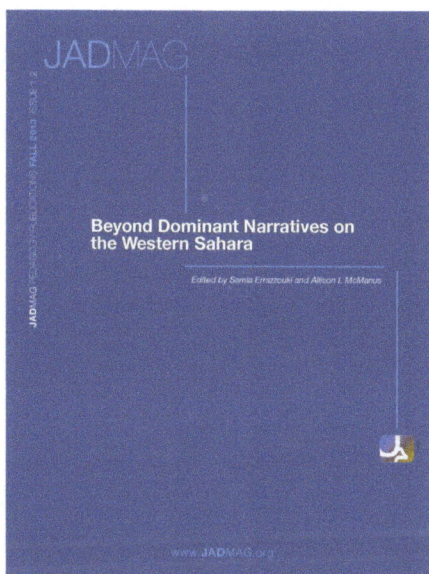

Gaza Revisited

Print copy $7.99
Electronic copy $5.49

This pedagogy publication examines the November 2012 military offensive and unpacks historical legacies, legal questions, media portrayals, and political considerations. In doing so, the publication helps create a context for the attack and considers possibilities for the future of the conflict and the balance of power in the Middle East more generally. The contributions situate a conflict that becomes acutely narrow during recurring instances of military confrontation.

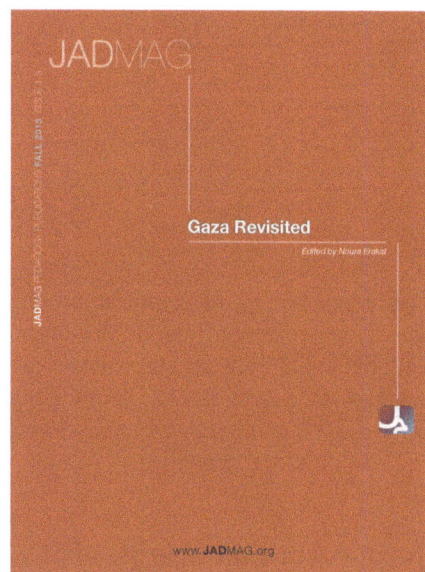

To purchase JadMags, visit www.tadweenpublishing.com

"Resistance Everywhere": The Gezi Protests and Dissident Visions of Turkey

Print copy $10.99
Electronic copy $6.99

Despite the sophisticated, critical, and oft-politically engaged literature emerging from and about the Arabian Peninsula, the region remains marginalized, in multiple ways, within academic and popular analyses. This JadMag addresses the ways in which frameworks of knowledge production have not only obscured social realities there, but also contributed to their construction. Our roundtable contributors approach this project from a number of different disciplinary perspectives and theoretical standpoints.

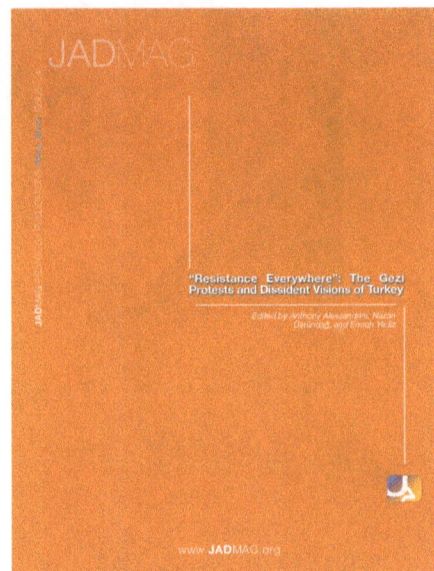

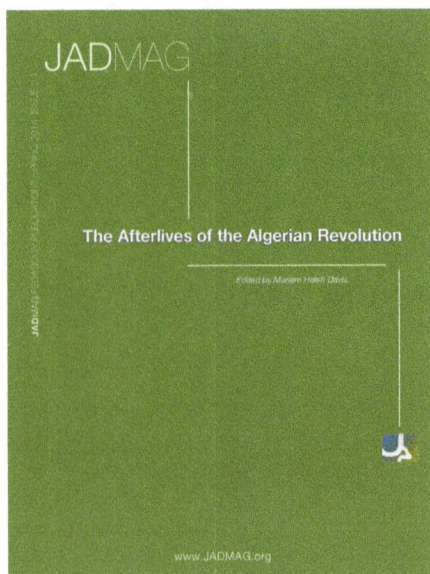

The Afterlives of the Algerian Revolution

Print copy $5.99
Electronic copy $3.49

In July 2012, Algeria celebrated its 50th anniversary of independence, which signaled the victory of the National Liberation Front over the French army. Despite five decades of Algerian independence, much of the work done on Algeria continues to focus on the colonial period. This pedagogical publication seeks to interrogate Algerian history since 1962 and considers how the revolution unleashed multiple socio-political dynamics that continue to mark contemporary Algeria.

Gaza in Context

Print Copy $6.99
Electronic Copy $4.99

This compendium, in combination with the pedagogical project Gaza in Context, uses Operation Protection Edge to demonstrate the temporal and spatial continuity of Israel's settler-colonial policies across Israel and the Occupied Territories in order to disrupt the language of exceptionalism surrounding Gaza today. The volume scrutinizes Israeli settler-colonialism through a multidisciplinary lens including history, law, development, political economy, and gender.

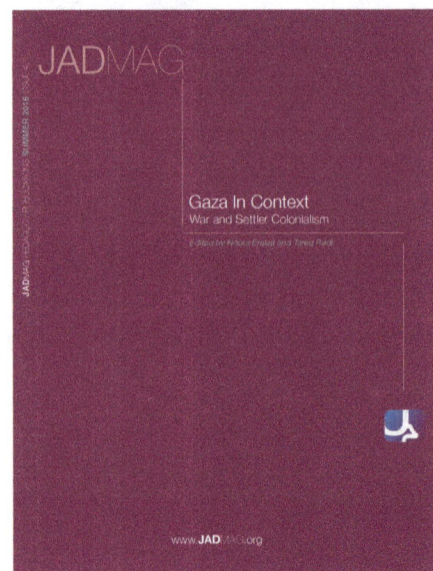

To purchase JadMags, visit **www.tadweenpublishing.com**